Enriched
Air Nitrox

DISCLAIMER:

The information contained in the SSI training materials is intended to give an individual enrolled in a training program a broad perspective of the diving activity. There are many recommendations and suggestions regarding the use of standard and specialized equipment for the activity. Not all of the equipment discussed in the training material can, or will, be used in this activity. The choice of equipment and techniques used in the program is determined by the location of the activity, the environmental conditions and other factors.

A choice of equipment and techniques cannot be made until the dive site is surveyed immediately prior to the dive. Based on the dive site, the decision should be made regarding which equipment and techniques shall be used. The decision belongs to the dive professional and the individual enrolled in the training program.

The intent of all SSI training materials is to give individuals as much information as possible in order for individuals to make their own decisions regarding the diving activity, what equipment should be used and what specific techniques may be needed. The ultimate decision on when and how to dive is for the individual diver to make.

First Edition
   First Printing, 11/96
   Second Printing, 3/98
   Third Printing, 9/99
   Fourth Printing, 10/02

Third Edition
   First Printing, 3/10

Second Edition
   First Printing, 6/04
      Revised 12/06
   Second Printing, 1/07

PRINTED IN THE USA

This manual is printed using Low-VOC ink.

www.diveSSI.com

Contents

Appendix

Acknowledgements

Editor in Chief	Doug McNeese
Writer	Watson DeVore, Harry Averill, R.J. Hartman, Doug McNeese, Steve Newman, Guido Wätzig
Manager of Development	Suzanne Fletcher
Graphic Designers	Lori Evans, Jennifer Silos
Cover Photo	Randy Pfizenmaier
Photographers	Lori Evans, Randy Pfizenmaier
Contributing Photographers	Black Durgeon, Wayne Hasson Paolo Lilla, Rick Murchison
Technical Editors	Paul Caputo, Mike Comsa, Larry Cox, Watson DeVore, Fred Good, Mike Huhn, Bruce Jameson, Robert Kennedy, Mike Kohut, Daryl Loller, Matt MacFarland, Kirk Mortensen, Frank Palmero, Eric Peterson, Mike Price, Kelvin Richards, Ed Salamone, Kim Volz, John Wall

Special thanks to Ikelite, Mike Huhn and the entire staff at Ocean Sports in San Carlos, Mexico.

Preface

You will see that each section includes several unique icons to highlight information or add information that relates to the text near it. In some cases, these icons point out information directly associated with the section objectives, while in other cases, the icon indicates a continuing education opportunity. While these icons are designed to help you learn and retain information, they also provide you with an easy reference to important information as you study.

Pearl

"Pearl" the oyster is found throughout the text to point out information that we believe is key to a new diver's success. The "pearls of wisdom" that our oyster friend highlights are designed to help you meet section objectives, assist in answering study guide questions and may be used in group discussions with your instructor.

Continuing Education

At Scuba Schools International, we believe that one of the keys to achieving and maintaining success as a diver is taking the "next step" via continuing education. To reinforce that belief, we have put a Continuing Education icon next to topics that correspond to continuing education opportunities available to you through your SSI Dive Center. Your SSI Instructor or Dive Center will be happy to answer any questions you may have about the continuing education programs listed throughout this manual.

Environment

SSI has always supported and promoted environmental awareness and believes that care for the environment should be a standard part of diver education from start to finish. For these reasons, an environmental icon has been included to highlight important environmental issues as they relate to divers and the underwater world. Topics that you will find the environmental icon next to include the importance of buoyancy control, reef appreciation and conservation, and using your equipment in an environmentally friendly way.

International Use

To meet international English language recommendations, some of the words you come across in this manual may look misspelled. The following is a list of these words in American English and their International counterparts.

American English	International Counterpart
Center	Centre
Meter	Metre
Gray	Grey
Aluminum	Aluminium

Throughout the manual, imperial measurements are listed first followed by the metric conversion. The following conversion units were used to convert the various measurements:

Conversions

1 ATA (Atmospheres Absolute) = 14.7 psi (pounds per square inch)
1 ATA = 1 bar
1 Metre = 3.28 feet
$C° = (F° -32) ÷ 1.8$
1 kg (kilogram) = 2.2 lbs (pounds)
1 km (kilometre) = .621 miles

Imperial

1 ATA = 33 fsw (feet of sea water)
1 ATA = 34 ffw (feet of fresh water)

Metric

1 BAR = 10 metres of sea water
1 BAR = 10.30 metres of fresh water

Note: For greater ease, many of the conversions in this text have been rounded to the nearest whole number, and may not reflect the exact conversion.

Be Ready for Your Journey

Welcome

Becoming a Nitrox Diver

Thank you for taking the first step in becoming a Nitrox Diver. This program is designed to be two distinct programs—SSI Enriched Air Nitrox Diver 32 and Enriched Air Nitrox Diver 40. Even if you decide that EAN32 fits the type of diving you will be doing, our suggestion is to complete the entire program. The more information you have, the more prepared you will be for your journey under water.

Enriched Air Nitrox Diver 32

If you're interested in longer bottom times and shorter surface intervals, then EAN32 is for you. As you will learn in this program, Enriched Air Nitrox can provide many benefits for recreational divers. Everything you need to know to dive Nitrox up to 32% is covered in the first 3 sections of this manual.

Enriched Air Nitrox Up to 40

If you're interested in learning much, much more and adding even more diving possibilities, then completing the entire program to dive up to EAN40 should be the goal.

Whatever you decide, we hope you enjoy learning all about Enriched Air Nitrox

Be Ready for Your Journey

All of our specialty programs are based on our signature training method—the SSI Diver Diamond. To become a comfortable and confident diver, it takes four ingredients:

Proper Knowledge

As in all SSI training programs, knowledge is power and replaces fears and fantasies with correct information. In this program, you will acquire the specific knowledge related to the Enriched Air Nitrox Specialty.

Proper Skills

Repetition is the mother of all skills. Under the guidance of your SSI Dive Professional, you will learn the information necessary to dive Enriched Air Nitrox.

Proper Equipment

The safest way to dive is in your own personally fitted Total Diving System. For this and all SSI Continuing Education programs, you may need additional equipment to perform these dives.

Proper Experience

Gaining the knowledge, skills and equipment necessary to complete dives using Nitrox is only one part of the journey. Going diving is the only way you can gain the actual experience needed to become a skilled Nitrox diver.

How Far Do You Want to Go?

If you believe the journey is just as important as the destination, then SSI's Continuing Education is for you. Taking specialties is a great way to hone your skills and learn some new ones. Continuing Education is exciting and limitless. It is your chance to begin exploring beyond the surface. Choose your personal combination of training and diving experience to reach your diving goals today!

SSI's Continuing Education programs are all menu-based home study programs. These specialty programs are designed so that you can learn at your own pace when it's convenient for you. Menu-based means you can take programs in a combined manner or one at a time based on your personal interest. Simply choose from specialties like Digital Underwater Photography, Deep Diving, Wreck Diving, Navigation, Night & Limited Visibility and you're on your way.

Getting involved is easy! If you're not sure which specialties you want to try, sign up for the Advanced Adventurer program. You will be able to take 5 dives and try 5 different specialties. Upon completion you will be recognized with an Advanced Adventurer card. These dives also count towards your rating if you choose to continue your training in one of the specialty areas covered.

For detailed information regarding SSI Specialty programs ask your local SSI Dive Center or visit www.diveSSI.com.

5 OR MORE LOGGED DIVES

LEVEL OF EXPERIENCE: 1

Complete the SSI Open Water Diver program & get this card!

12 OR MORE LOGGED DIVES

LEVEL OF EXPERIENCE: 2

Complete Level 2 dives & 2 Specialty Programs.

24 OR MORE LOGGED DIVES

LEVEL OF EXPERIENCE: 3

Complete Level 3 dives & 4 Specialty Programs.

50 OR MORE LOGGED DIVES

LEVEL OF EXPERIENCE: 4

Complete Level 4 dives, 4 Specialty Programs & the Diver Stress & Rescue Program.

AVAILABLE SPECIALTIES — *Take one or take them all!*

- Adaptive Scuba Diving
- Boat Diving
- Computer Diving
- Deep Diving
- Digital Underwater Photography
- Diver Stress & Rescue
- Dry Suit Diving
- Emergency Training
  - First Aid & CPR
  - Emergency Oxygen
  - AED
- Enriched Air Nitrox
- Equipment Techniques

- Navigation
- Night and Limited Visibility Diving
- Perfect Buoyancy
- Science of Diving
- Search & Recovery
- Technical Extended Range
  - Advanced Nitrox
  - Technical Foundations
  - Decompression Procedures
  - Advanced Decompression
  - Normoxic Trimix
- Waves, Tides & Currents
- Wreck Diving

You can become a Dive Professional once you have completed Level 4!
Ask your SSI Dive Center for complete details.

Instructor Levels

Quality Divers Start with Qualified Instructors

Other Instructor Programs

◇ Specialty Instructor
◇ Diver Stress & Rescue Instructor
◇ Enriched Air Nitrox Instructor
◇ Scuba Rangers Instructor
◇ Technical Extended Range
  – Advanced Nitrox Instructor
  – Technical Foundations Instructor
  – Decompression Procedures Instructor
  – Advanced Decompression Procedures Instructor
  – Normoxic Trimix Instructor
  – TechXR Instructor Trainer

REWARDS FOR EXPERIENCE

No Training Required!

Taking a specific number of specialties and continuing your pursuit of dives allows you to earn higher levels of diver ratings. SSI Ratings are the only ratings in the industry that combine training and experience requirements, proving that SSI Ratings are truly earned.

Reward yourself as you reach new milestones in your diving adventures!

Intro

About SSI

Scuba Schools International grew out of the passion of a few avid divers who were intent on making it possible for anyone to learn to scuba dive.

SSI provides education materials, dive training and scuba certification for divers, dive instructors, dive centers and dive resorts around the world. Since 1970, SSI has expanded to 27 International Offices, doing business in 110 countries with training materials in 25 languages representing over 2,400 dive centers and resorts. SSI Certification Cards are welcomed all over the planet, wherever you choose to dive.

Scuba Schools International is clearly a name you can trust in the diving community and we attribute that success to uncompromising standards and a focus on quality not quantity.

Involvement

As well as being an industry leader, SSI is also a founding member of the industry's standards body in the USA and abroad—in the USA, it's the RSTC (Recreational Scuba Training Council) and in Europe, it's the WRSTC and the EU (European Standards—EN 14153-1-3 for divers and 144413-1-2 for scuba instructors).

Reward Yourself. You Deserve It

Becoming certified in Enriched Air Nitrox is an achievement. Be sure to reward yourself for reaching this major milestone with an SSI Enriched Air Nitrox certification card. This is an opportunity to commemorate your hard-earned accomplishment.

Where to Go From Here.

We are certain that your journey through Enriched Air Nitrox will be everything you imagined and more. Don't forget you can always combine other specialties to increase your diving knowledge—the possibilities are limitless. Now, let's go have some fun!

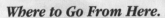

Your Introduction to Nitrox (EANx)

Section 1 Objectives
After completing this section you will be able to:

◆ State the definition of Enriched Air Nitrox (EANx),

◆ Describe the benefits of nitrox,

◆ List the limitations of nitrox.

O f all the advances in recreational sport diving, perhaps none generates more excitement than the use of Enriched Air Nitrox (EANx). The term EANx has been shortened to nitrox. Yes, nitrox sounds like Voodoo gas, but it's quite the contrary. The major benefit to diving with nitrox is the gas that limits our depth and time—nitrogen. Nitrox has a higher concentration of oxygen and a lower concentration of nitrogen. This alone adds additional diver safety by using this gas and staying within the recreational sport diving limits.

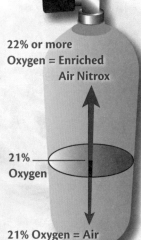

22% or more Oxygen = Enriched Air Nitrox

21% Oxygen

21% Oxygen = Air

Enriched Air Nitrox

Nitrox was introduced as the gas of the future in the early 90's, but it took many years for dive centers, resorts and live-aboard dive boats to catch up with specialized compressors to offer nitrox. However with nearly every advance in diving, these gains are not without their limitations. So in this section we will let you know exactly what nitrox is and how we can use it in our diving adventures.

The Composition of the Air We Breathe

As you learned in your Open Water program, the air we breathe is compressed air. Compressed air is no different than the air we breathe every day with one exception, all impurities have been filtered out and the air is placed inside a scuba cylinder. Compressed air is mainly 79% nitrogen and 21% oxygen.

What is Nitrox?

Simply stated, nitrox is any mixture of nitrogen and oxygen — thus the term NITROX. That also means that the air you are breathing right now is one form of nitrox.

DIVER DIAMOND
KNOWLEDGE · SKILLS · EQUIPMENT · EXPERIENCE
SSI

22% or more Oxygen = Enriched Air Nitrox

21% Oxygen

For simplicity, we use the term *nitrox* and the acronym *EANx* solely to refer to mixtures with oxygen concentrations (FO_2) of 22 percent or more. Whenever we use the term *air*, we are referring solely to a mixture of approximately 79 percent nitrogen and 21 percent oxygen.

Divers generally use the terms *Enriched Air, Enriched Air Nitrox, nitrox* and the acronym *EANx* interchangeably.

EANx is an acronym for *Enriched Air Nitrox* in which the x is a variable standing for the FO_2 value. Thus EAN32, for example, represents a nitrox mixture with an FO_2 of 32 percent.

Nitrox I and II

While the two most commonly used nitrox mixtures in recreational diving are EAN32 and EAN36, this program will teach you the use of nitrox up to 40%.

EAN32 is well suited for most recreational dives. Divers can use EAN32 at any depth within the recommended depth limit for recreational diving (100 feet/ 30 metres).

EAN36 is an excellent gas for extended dives at moderate depths. At shallower depths, EAN36 allows longer bottom times without decompression. However, as you approach the recommended depth limit for recreational diving (100 feet/30 metres), the higher concentration of oxygen in EAN36 puts recreational divers at greater risk. The risks of EAN36 will be discussed in Section 2.

21%

79%

OXYGEN

32%

36%

NITROGEN

68%

64%

AIR

EAN32   **EAN36**

The composition of AIR, EAN32 and EAN36, the three most popular breathing gases for recreational divers.

This manual covers the use of nitrox mixtures with oxygen concentrations ranging from 22 to 40%. In most instances, it is unlikely you will dive mixtures "greater" than EAN32.

Note: The use of nitrox above EAN40 is beyond recreational sport diving. If you are interested in going beyond the sports diving limits, ask your SSI Instructor about enrolling in the SSI Technical Extended Range program.

Using Nitrox

Over the last two decades, the way people dive has changed dramatically. In the early days of recreational diving, everything was based on dive tables and square profiles—descend, swim along the bottom and ascend. In order to avoid decompression, square profiles limited dive time under water.

Today, with the introduction of dive computers, we dive multi-level profiles. Multi-level diving gives you greater bottom time while staying within the no-decompression limits. Diving nitrox adds a lot of benefits to multi-level computer diving.

A common misconception is that nitrox enables divers to go deeper than they can on air. While nitrox has benefits, it also has limitations. A complete understanding of the benefits and limitations will help you decide whether to dive nitrox or air.

The Advantages of Nitrox

Nitrox offers divers these potential benefits:

More Bottom Time. Because nitrox contains less nitrogen than air, breathing nitrox is the equivalent of diving air at substantially shallower depths, e.g.—EAN32 is 32% oxygen and 68% nitrogen.

Diving EANx has the potential to provide longer no-decompression limits, shorter surface intervals and longer repetitive dives. This fact is well documented and considered by many to be the primary benefit of using nitrox.

Improved Safety. Diving nitrox exposes your body to less nitrogen than diving air at the same depth. If you dive nitrox using the same depth and time limitations with an air table or air computer you can reduce the risk of decompression sickness. This forgoes the benefit of more bottom time, longer no-decompression limits, shorter surface intervals and longer repetitive dives.

Less Fatigue. Some people believe that breathing greater concentrations of oxygen when diving nitrox, your body is less fatigued and you might even feel slightly energized. There is no medical evidence to support this theory.

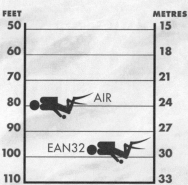

In terms of avoiding decompression sickness, breathing nitrox is the equivalent of diving air at substantially shallower depths.

The Limitations of Nitrox

Diving nitrox is not without a few limitations:

Nitrox Use Requires Additional Training. There are a number of things you must learn before you can use nitrox correctly. Some can be learned through home-study, while others require the guidance and supervision of a qualified instructor.

Nitrox Use May Require Special Equipment. The dive equipment you presently own may or may not be suitable for use with nitrox. Some items may require special preparation and modification. Other items may need to be replaced by equipment specifically designed for use with EANx. There may be yet additional items you must acquire, such as oxygen analyzers that are simply not necessary when diving air.

Nitrox May Not Always Be Readily Available. Despite its surge in popularity, nitrox is still not available at some dive resorts and live aboard dive vessels. Additionally, not all domestic dive stores offer nitrox. This situation is changing rapidly, but you still cannot count on having access to nitrox everywhere you go.

Entails Additional Risk. When diving nitrox, there is a risk of oxygen toxicity which we will discuss in Section 2 that is simply not present when diving air within recreational limits. Training can help you better manage or overcome this risk, but like all risks, it can never be totally eliminated.

Compared to air, the use of nitrox by recreational divers is still relatively new. Not surprisingly, there are a number of misunderstandings regarding nitrox. Among them:

Some Divers Mistakenly Believe That Nitrox is Designed for Ultra-Deep Diving. Ironically, nitrox has more severe depth limitations than air.

Another Misconception is that Diving Nitrox is Substantially More Dangerous Than Diving Air. Diving nitrox exposes divers to some risks that are not present when diving air within recreational diving limits. It may also reduce some of the risks associated with air diving. With proper training and equipment, the additional risks inherent in diving EANx can be managed to the point where they are offset by nitrox's potential benefits. In this respect, nitrox diving is no different than any other diving activity.

A common misconception is that nitrox enables divers to go deeper than they can on air.

History of Nitrox

Nitrox is not new. The blending of oxygen began in the 17th century. Since then Enriched Air Nitrox has been used in various applications for medicine and commercial diving. Even the diving pioneers of this century have used nitrox as a breathing gas to shorten decompression time. No gas has been researched as thoroughly as oxygen. For this reason, nitrox is considered to be safe.

Summary

This section gave you a brief introduction into nitrox, its benefits and its limitations. In choosing to dive nitrox, you must decide which of these potential benefits are more important. If your objective is to add an extra safety margin to your diving, then simply dive your no-decompression limits with an air table or air computer. If your objective is to maximize bottom time, diving EANx provides longer no-decompression limits, shorter surface intervals and longer repetitive dives. We will discuss these objectives at greater length in Section 2 when we take a closer look at the affects of nitrox on your body.

Section 1 Review Questions

1. We use the term nitrox and the acronym EANx solely to refer to mixtures with oxygen concentrations (FO_2) of _____ _____ ____ _____.

2. Compressed air is mainly ____% _____ and ____% _____.

3. The two most commonly used nitrox mixtures in recreational diving are _____ and _____ .

4. Because nitrox contains less _____ than air, breathing nitrox is the equivalent of diving air at substantially _____ depths.

5. Diving EANx has the potential to provide _____ -_____ limits, _____ - _____ intervals and _____ _____ dives.

6. The _____ - _____ you presently own may or may not be _____ for use with nitrox.

7. A common _____ is that nitrox enables divers to _____ _____ than they can on air.

Nitrox,
Your Body
and the
Underwater
World

2

2

Section 2 Objectives
After completing this section you will be able to:

♦ List the effects of breathing more oxygen,

♦ State the benefits of breathing less nitrogen,

♦ Recognize the signs and symptoms of CNS oxygen toxicity,

♦ Understand how to prevent CNS oxygen toxicity.

Diving nitrox exposes your body to more oxygen than diving air at similar depths. It is important to understand how this could affect your health and safety. It also influences the way you plan and conduct your dives. You will discover that while breathing less nitrogen offers potential benefits, breathing more oxygen presents additional considerations.

Breathing More Oxygen

When you first learned to dive, you may have been told that breathing pure oxygen at depth could be toxic. This is not entirely true. Oxygen toxicity depends on factors such as the increased percentage of oxygen and the depth and length of that exposure.

Breathing nitrox exposes us to considerably more oxygen than air, e.g.—EAN32 contains 50 percent more oxygen than air. This means that while oxygen toxicity is not a concern when diving air within the recreational sport diving depths, the same may not be true for nitrox.

To understand this whole subject better, we must review the concept of partial pressure. Once you understand how to calculate oxygen and nitrogen concentrations in a gas mixture you will also be able to manage both in your dive planning.

The Concept of Partial Pressure

The concept of partial pressure deals with the fraction of each of the gases which can be found in a gas mixture. For example, as we know from Section 1, air consists of 79% nitrogen and 21% oxygen. At one (1) atmosphere the partial pressure of each of gas found in air adds up to 1 atmosphere as well. In this example the partial pressure of nitrogen is .79 atmospheres absolute and the partial pressure of oxygen is .21 atmospheres absolute. Partial pressure is the best way to compare the levels of oxygen found in any mixture of the air we breathe under water—nitrox or air. The partial pressure of oxygen is abbreviated ppO_2, or simply PO_2.

What, Exactly, Does PO_2 Mean?

Simply stated, it is a numerical value you obtain by multiplying ambient pressure (expressed as depth in atmospheres or bar) by the fraction of oxygen (FO_2) found in the breathing gas. Example, EAN32 at one (1) atmosphere, the partial pressure of oxygen is .32 atmospheres absolute.

Equivalent Air Depth (EAD) is the best way to compare the amount of nitrogen found in nitrox with that found in air. We will explain EAD later in this section.

The risk of CNS oxygen toxicity becomes more substantial above a PO_2 of 1.4 atmospheres. Increasingly, experts recommend a limiting PO_2 of 1.4 atmospheres for all divers. You can always choose a more conservative approach and limit your PO_2 exposure to lesser values.

The example below compares the PO_2 levels of air and those required to sustain consciousness and life by limiting PO_2 levels for diving. You will see that these values cover quite a range.

Partial Pressure of Oxygen (PO_2) Levels

PO_2	Description
0.10	Minimum PO_2 level required to sustain life
0.12	Minimum PO_2 level required to maintain consciousness (approximate)
0.16	Threshold for hypoxia (exercise tolerance and mental performance diminishes below this level)
0.21	Normal PO_2 level of air
1.10	Threshold for oxygen toxicity symptoms
1.40	PO_2 level at which oxygen presents a moderate risk to divers (Recommended limiting PO_2 for recreational divers)
1.60	PO_2 level at which oxygen presents a more substantial risk to divers (Absolute limiting PO_2 for recreational divers)

At what depths are you likely to encounter these limiting PO$_2$ values? This will depend on the FO$_2$ of the mixture you are breathing.

Partial Pressure of Oxygen (PO$_2$)
Based on Depth and Fraction of Oxygen (FO$_2$)

Depth Feet	21%	22%	23%	24%	25%	26%	27%	28%	29%	30%	31%	32%	33%	34%	35%	36%
35	0.42	0.44	0.46	0.48	0.50	0.52	0.54	0.56	0.58	0.60	0.62	0.64	0.66	0.68	0.70	0.72
40	0.46	0.48	0.51	0.53	0.55	0.57	0.59	0.62	0.64	0.66	0.68	0.70	0.73	0.75	0.77	0.79
50	0.53	0.55	0.58	0.60	0.63	0.65	0.68	0.70	0.73	0.75	0.78	0.80	0.83	0.85	0.88	0.90
60	0.59	0.62	0.64	0.67	0.70	0.73	0.76	0.78	0.81	0.84	0.87	0.90	0.92	0.95	0.98	1.01
70	0.65	0.68	0.71	0.74	0.78	0.81	0.84	0.87	0.90	0.93	0.96	0.99	1.02	1.05	1.09	1.12
80	0.71	0.75	0.78	0.82	0.85	0.88	0.92	0.95	0.99	1.02	1.05	1.09	1.12	1.16	1.19	1.22
90	0.78	0.81	0.85	0.89	0.93	0.96	1.00	1.04	1.07	1.11	1.15	1.18	1.22	1.26	1.30	1.33
100	0.84	0.88	0.92	0.96	1.00	1.04	1.08	1.12	1.16	1.20	1.24	1.28	1.32	1.36	1.40	1.44
110	0.90	0.95	0.99	1.03	1.08	1.12	1.16	1.20	1.25	1.29	1.33	1.38	1.42	1.46	1.51	1.55
120	0.97	1.01	1.06	1.10	1.15	1.20	1.24	1.29	1.33	1.38	1.43	1.47	1.52	1.56		
130	1.03	1.08	1.13	1.18	1.23	1.27	1.32	1.37	1.42	1.47	1.52	1.57				

Partial Pressure of Oxygen (PO$_2$)
Based on Depth and Fraction of Oxygen (FO$_2$)

Depth Metres	21%	22%	23%	24%	25%	26%	27%	28%	29%	30%	31%	32%	33%	34%	35%	36%
10	0.42	0.44	0.46	0.48	0.50	0.52	0.54	0.56	0.58	0.60	0.62	0.64	0.66	0.68	0.70	0.72
12	0.48	0.48	0.51	0.53	0.55	0.57	0.59	0.62	0.64	0.66	0.68	0.70	0.73	0.75	0.77	0.79
15	0.53	0.55	0.58	0.60	0.63	0.65	0.68	0.70	0.73	0.75	0.78	0.80	0.83	0.85	0.88	0.90
18	0.59	0.62	0.64	0.67	0.70	0.73	0.76	0.78	0.81	0.84	0.87	0.90	0.92	0.95	0.98	1.01
21	0.65	0.68	0.71	0.74	0.78	0.81	0.84	0.87	0.90	0.93	0.95	0.99	1.02	1.05	1.09	1.12
24	0.71	0.75	0.78	0.82	0.85	0.88	0.92	0.95	0.99	1.02	1.05	1.09	1.12	1.16	1.19	1.22
27	0.78	0.81	0.85	0.89	0.93	0.96	1.00	1.04	1.07	1.11	1.15	1.18	1.22	1.26	1.30	1.33
30	0.84	0.88	0.92	0.96	1.00	1.04	1.08	1.12	1.16	1.20	1.24	1.28	1.32	1.36	1.40	1.44
34	0.92	0.97	1.01	1.06	1.10	1.14	1.19	1.23	1.28	1.32	1.36	1.41	1.45	1.50	1.54	1.58
37	0.99	1.03	1.08	1.13	1.18	1.22	1.27	1.32	1.36	1.41	1.46	1.50	1.55	1.60		
40	1.05	1.10	1.15	1.20	1.25	1.30	1.35	1.40	1.45	1.50	1.55	1.60				

PO$_2$ levels vary by depth and FO$_2$. Shaded areas indicate PO$_2$ values in excess of 1.4 atmospheres. Divers should avoid exposing themselves to PO$_2$ levels in these ranges.

The tables on page 2-4 show how PO_2 levels vary by depth and FO_2. By examining these numbers, you will see that "lean" nitrox mixtures carry a reduced risk of oxygen toxicity. As FO_2 approach and exceed 32 percent, however, PO_2 levels rise.

This table also helps illustrate why EAN32 is the recommended nitrox mixture for most recreational dives. If you remain within the generally recommended recreational depth limit of 100 feet/30 metres of the surface you will have an extra 10 feet/3 metres safety margin before you exceed a PO_2 of 1.4 atmospheres. You would have to descend to 132 feet/40 metres before you exceed a PO_2 of 1.6.

| Partial Pressure of Oxygen (PO_2) | = | Depth in Atmospheres | X | Fraction of Oxygen (FO_2) |

FEET

$$PO_2 = \left[\left(\frac{Depth}{33\ ft}\right) + 1\right] \times FO_2$$

METRES

$$PO_2 = \left[\left(\frac{Depth}{10\ m}\right) + 1\right] \times FO_2$$

The formulas for determining partial pressure of oxygen (PO_2). Use the top formula for feet; the bottom formula for metres.

How to Calculate Partial Pressure of Oxygen (PO_2)

The formulas for determining the partial pressure of oxygen (PO_2) appear in the diagram to the left.

In this formula, *Depth* is a variable representing either feet or metres of salt water. The portion of the equation in brackets, by itself, can be used to determine absolute depth in either atmospheres or bar.

Limiting PO_2

At what PO_2 can oxygen become toxic? This depends on a variety of factors.

As with decompression sickness, susceptibility to O_2 toxicity varies from person to person and from day to day. Factors such as physical exertion and carbon dioxide levels may also affect the onset of oxygen toxicity symptoms.

The threshold for CNS oxygen toxicity appears to be 1.1 atmospheres. However, even though convulsions caused by oxygen toxicity can occur at this level, it is extremely unlikely divers will experience them — if they keep their total exposure to PO_2 in the range of 1.1 to 1.4 atmospheres, and within the time limits discussed later in this section.

Depth in Atmospheres	X	Fraction of Oxygen (FO_2)	=	Partial Pressure of Oxygen (PO_2)
4.0	X	0.21	=	0.84
4.0	X	0.32	=	1.28

The Benefits of Breathing Less Nitrogen

The examples above show how using the equation described earlier, we determine the PO_2 for air and EAN32 at a depth of 100 feet/ 30 metres. Note that with EAN32, the PO_2 is over 50 percent greater than it is for air.

When diving EAN*x*, you expose your body to less overall nitrogen than would occur were you making the same dive breathing air. Among the best ways to examine just how much less nitrogen you expose your body to is through the concept of Equivalent Air Depth, or EAD which we will deal with in Section 4.

The fact that diving nitrox exposes divers to less nitrogen when diving at the same depth when using air or the same overall level of nitrogen as diving air at shallower depths, brings several intriguing possibilities to mind.

Nitrox Use and Bottom Time

Can you use nitrox to gain longer bottom times? Absolutely! In fact, this is what many consider to be among the greatest benefits of diving nitrox. Coupled with longer bottom times, you may also enjoy shorter surface intervals and longer repetitive dives — just as you would if diving air at shallower depths.

The methodologies for doing so are fairly straightforward. For example, you can simply use the equivalent air depth values for any given nitrox mixture with the same air-based dive tables you normally use. You can also use special nitrox dive tables or air- or nitrox-based dive computers. We cover how to do so in Section 4.

Nitrox and Nitrogen Narcosis

The fact that diving nitrox exposes divers to less nitrogen, suggests the use of nitrox should result in less nitrogen narcosis. Studies have not been able to verify this, however. A possible reason why is that oxygen itself can be narcotic, and exposure to greater concentrations of oxygen, such as occurs when diving nitrox, may also cause impairment.

Until such time as researchers can verify what impact, if any, nitrox has on narcosis, you should not count on experiencing less narcosis or impairment when diving nitrox than you do when diving air at comparable depths.

Nitrox Use and Decompression Sickness

Can you use nitrox to reduce the risk of decompression sickness? Absolutely! Let us assume we do the same diving profile on air and on nitrox. Nitrox contains a smaller percentage of nitrogen in comparison to air. Therefore, less nitrogen will be absorbed by the body when using nitrox instead of using air.

To add an additional safety margin using nitrox, simply use your dive computer with air settings. Diving EAN32 can be safely performed to a maximum depth of 100 feet/ 30 metres. Diving EAN32 takes into account the MOD (maximum operating depth) and CNS (central nervous system) limits. This is exactly why SSI designed the Enriched Air Nitrox Diver 32%.

Over the years, both the US Navy Dive Tables and similar dive-planning tools derived from the Navy Tables have proven themselves well suited for use by recreational divers. When remaining within recommended dive-table limits, the incidence of decompression sickness among such divers is less than one percent. Still, no dive table or dive computer — even though used correctly — can guarantee divers will not suffer decompression sickness.

For this reason, experts encourage recreational divers to build in additional safety factors when using dive tables and computers. Such steps may include:

Using more conservative no-decompression limits, such as the Doppler no-stop limits appearing on the SSI Dive Tables.

◆ Not "pushing" either dive tables or dive computers to their absolute limits.

◆ Making slower ascents than those dictated by the dive table or computer being used.

◆ Making safety stops.

The "Sacrifice" of the Nitrox Safety Margin

As already stated, many nitrox divers like to use the fact that EAN*x* contains less nitrogen than air to gain an additional safety margin to avoid decompression sickness. They treat nitrox as though it was air, using the same dive tables or dive computer they would if actually breathing air. Doing so means sacrificing the advantages nitrox offers in terms of longer bottom times, shorter surface intervals and longer repetitive dives.

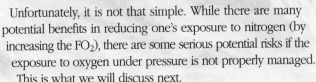

While treating nitrox as though it were air, may somewhat reduce the risk of decompression sickness, *it does not eliminate it*. Additionally, divers who treat nitrox as air must still keep their exposure to elevated partial pressures of oxygen within acceptable limits.

Is Richer Better?

As discussed earlier, the shallower the equivalent air depth, the higher the FO_2. This might lead one to conclude that you can achieve the greatest benefit from nitrox by diving the richest mix possible. In fact, why not go all the way and dive pure oxygen? After all, with respect to exposure to nitrogen, diving pure O_2 always yields an equivalent air depth that is theoretically above that of sea level.

Unfortunately, it is not that simple. While there are many potential benefits in reducing one's exposure to nitrogen (by increasing the FO_2), there are some serious potential risks if the exposure to oxygen under pressure is not properly managed. This is what we will discuss next.

CNS Oxygen Toxicity

Oxygen, while essential to life, is nevertheless toxic at elevated levels. Were it not for our bodies' chemical defense mechanisms, oxygen would cause undesirable chemical reactions resulting in cell death. At atmospheric pressure, our normal defense mechanisms offset the toxic effects of oxygen. However, at depth the increased partial pressure of oxygen in the gases divers breathe can overwhelm these defense mechanisms and result in oxygen toxicity. While oxygen can be toxic to all body tissues, its most noticeable and immediate effects take place in the lungs and central nervous system.

Pulmonary Oxygen Toxicity. Also called the Lorrain Smith Effect—develops when humans breathe gases containing oxygen at partial pressures of 0.5 atmospheres or more. However, the length of time to which people must expose themselves to such gases before symptoms of pulmonary oxygen toxicity arise is well beyond the duration of most sport dives. Thus, it poses no real risk to recreational divers.

Central Nervous System (CNS) Oxygen Toxicity. Also called the Paul Bert Effect—is of more concern. This is because once CNS oxygen toxicity symptoms develop, they may progress rapidly to convulsions.

Interestingly enough, CNS oxygen toxicity is not necessarily fatal by itself. The problem is, under water a CNS "hit" could cause a diver to lose consciousness or the ability to maintain second-stage regulator/airway control. Consequently, what might be a non-fatal CNS oxygen toxicity episode on dry land, can easily lead to death by drowning under water.

Contributing Factors. Several factors may contribute to CNS oxygen toxicity. Obviously, exceeding recommended limiting PO$_2$ is one such factor. Another factor is length of exposure.

James Lorrain Smith 1862 to 1931

Studied Medicine and Arts at Edinburgh University — The Lorrain Smith Effect was named after him as an honor to his scientific work.

Paul Bert 1833 to 1886

Published several studies regarding the effects of pressure to the human body and he was the one discovering the role of nitrogen in decompression — The Paul Bert Effect was named after him as an honor to his scientific work.

DIVER DIAMOND
SSI
KNOWLEDGE · SKILLS · EXPERIENCE · EQUIPMENT

The greater your total oxygen "dose," as determined by a combination of depth and time, the greater the likelihood of a CNS "hit."

Another factor that may contribute to CNS oxygen toxicity is elevated carbon dioxide levels. This may result from exertion or from using an inadequate or poorly maintained Air Delivery System ADS.

Recently, evidence has been presented that the active ingredient in many over-the-counter decongestants, as well as other drugs, may act as "O_2 exciters"—agents that accelerate the onset of CNS oxygen toxicity. Of course the best way to avoid such risks is to refrain from taking any drugs while diving, unless specifically approved by a licensed Medical Practitioner specializing in diving medicine.

Recognizing and Responding to CNS Oxygen Toxicity.
Since CNS oxygen toxicity is among the greatest of risks in nitrox diving, you must be able to recognize its warning signs and symptoms, both in yourself and others, and respond appropriately.

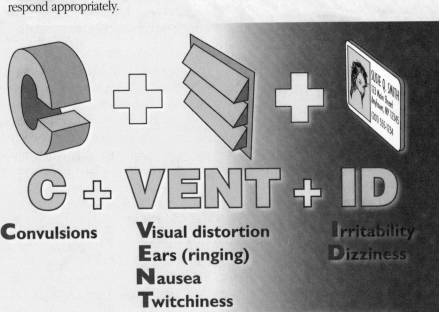

C + VENT + ID

Convulsions **V**isual distortion **I**rritability
Ears (ringing) **D**izziness
Nausea
Twitchiness

An easy way to memorize the primary signs and symptoms of CNS oxygen toxicity.

The diagram above depicts how many divers remember the signs and symptoms of CNS oxygen toxicity. (A sign is something we see in others; a symptom is something we experience ourselves.)

The chief sign of oxygen toxicity is convulsions. A diver suffering from convulsions may be unable to keep a second-stage regulator in his or her mouth, and may be unable to prevent himself or herself from inhaling water. Such a diver is in immediate risk of death by drowning.

If you notice any of the symptoms of CNS oxygen toxicity, signal your buddy and begin an immediate, but controlled ascent.

In addition, a diver suffering from CNS oxygen toxicity may be unable to stop whatever he or she is doing. For example, a diver may continue swimming horizontally, despite wanting to stop. It is as though his or her muscles do not listen to the brain. (Experimental subjects in oxygen limit testing often say they experience this sensation just before convulsing.) Affected divers may also be unresponsive to attempts to communicate or appear unusually irritable.

Any of the *symptoms* of oxygen toxicity should act as a warning that we need to take immediate action before convulsions and loss of consciousness occur.

C + VENT + ID — The symptoms of CNS oxygen toxicity include:

◆ **Convulsions**

◆ **Visual Distortion** — Any impairment in vision, including "tunnel" vision.

◆ **Ears** — Any changes in normal hearing function, especially a "ringing" sensation.

◆ **Nausea** — This may vary in severity and be intermittent.

◆ **Twitchiness** — Muscle spasms of any kind, especially in facial muscles.

◆ **Irritability** — Uncharacteristic personality changes, anxiety and confusion (as mentioned earlier, this is also a sign).

◆ **Dizziness** — Vertigo or disorientation.

An easy way to memorize the primary signs and symptoms of CNS oxygen toxicity.

Any manifestation of the signs and symptoms of CNS oxygen toxicity requires an immediate response. The focus of that response should be reducing the affected diver's exposure to oxygen by ascending.

If you notice these symptoms in yourself, signal your buddy and begin an immediate, but controlled ascent. Although moving to shallow water should bring a rapid cessation of symptoms, the most prudent response will be to continue the ascent, make a normal safety stop, then end the dive.

Upon surfacing, carefully analyze what went wrong. Were oxygen limits exceeded? Was the nitrox mixture incorrectly used, analyzed or labeled? Are there any other factors that might account for the episode?

It is important to realize that one cannot determine precisely from symptoms whether they were due to oxygen toxicity or some other factor. For example, while facial twitching is a strong indicator of oxygen toxicity, other symptoms such as nausea and vertigo may be due to any of a wide variety of factors.

Check with a Physician

Whether or not symptoms of oxygen toxicity can be tied conclusively to diver error, it may still be best to discuss the episode with a qualified diving physician before diving again.

If CNS oxygen toxicity manifests itself in convulsions, there may not be much the convulsing diver can do about it. At this point, the affected diver will be dependent on the prompt and appropriate response by an observant dive buddy.

If you see your buddy or another diver begin to convulse, hold the diver in place until the convulsions cease, then begin a slow, controlled ascent. If, after holding the affected diver in place for approximately 15 seconds the convulsions do not stop, go ahead and bring the convulsing diver to the surface at as controlled a rate as you can.

Admittedly, this is a tough call. A convulsing diver may be blocking his or her airway, and thus be at risk of experiencing a lung overpressure injury during ascent. Yet, if a diver is allowed to remain in a convulsive state at depth, he or she may drown.

After the tonic phase of a convulsion ceases, the diver is said to be post-ictal. This means the diver is unconscious, but

not convulsive. At this point, the diver should gradually regain consciousness, reaching full alertness within 10 minutes.

If he or she does not regain consciousness, you should suspect cerebral gas embolism and act accordingly.

Regardless of what actions the situation dictates, be sure to alert the responding Emergency Medical System (EMS) personnel, and the emergency room physician, that the affected diver may have had a reaction to elevated partial pressures of oxygen.

Preventing CNS Oxygen Toxicity

The best way to deal with CNS oxygen toxicity is to prevent it. Steps that may help you do so include:

♦ **Establishing and Remaining Within Maximum Operating Depth (MOD) Limits.**

♦ **Limiting Depth.** The shallower you remain, the less risk there is of oxygen toxicity. Ask yourself: Is it absolutely necessary to spend the entire dive in the sand? Or, are there as many things to see near the top of the wreck or reef?

♦ **Reducing CO_2 Levels.** There are several steps you can take to reduce the level of carbon dioxide (CO_2) in your body and, thus, your susceptibility to oxygen toxicity.

♦ **Plan Your Dive So That It Requires the Least Possible Exertion.** Avoid strong currents and long travel distances.

♦ **Use Only Adequate, Well-Maintained Second-Stage Regulators.** The easier your second-stage regulators breathe, the less CO_2 build-up you will experience. Be sure to discuss the suitability of any second-stage regulators you currently own or are considering purchasing for nitrox diving with your SSI Dive Center.

♦ **Breathe Slowly and Deeply.** This maximizes gas exchange in your lungs and body air spaces, and further reduces CO_2 levels. Do not skip breathe. If you have difficulty breathing, remember to stop, breathe deeply, think, then act.

In terms of susceptibility to oxygen toxicity, the actual variation among individuals, or from one day to the next, may be as great as 13:1. Fortunately, NOAA's working-diver limits are conservative and — while they cannot guarantee 100 percent safety — they nonetheless substantially increase one's safety margin.

Maximum Operating Depth (MOD)

Every time you dive nitrox, you should first establish a Maximum Operating Depth or MOD. Exactly what this MOD will be will depend on the concentration of oxygen in the gas you will breathe, and the limiting PO_2 you choose to remain within.

Maximum Operating Depths (MODs)
Based on Fraction or Oxygen (FO_2) and Limiting PO_2 of 1.3-1.6 ATA/Bar • Depths in Feet and Metres

Limiting PO_2	21%	22%	23%	24%	25%	26%	27%	28%	29%	30%	31%	32%	33%	34%	35%	36%
DEPTH IN FEET OF SALT WATER																
1.3	171	162	153	145	138	132	125	120	114	110	105	101	97	93	89	86
1.4	187	177	167	159	151	144	138	132	126	121	116	111	107	102	99	95
1.5	202	192	182	173/52	165	157	150	143	137	132	126	121	117	112	108	104
1.6	218	207	196	187	178	170	162	155	149	143	137	132	127	122	117	113
DEPTH IN METRES OF SALT WATER																
1.3	52	49	47	44	42	40	38	36	35	33	32	31	29	28	27	26
1.4	57	54	51	48	46	44	42	40	38	37	35	33	32	31	30	29
1.5	61	58	55	53	50	48	46	44	42	40	38	37	35	34	33	32
1.6	66	63	60	57	54	52	49	47	45	43	42	40	38	37	36	34

Shaded areas represent PO_2 levels in excess of 1.4 atmospheres. Experts increasingly recommend avoiding depths that will expose divers to partial pressures of oxygen in these ranges.

The table above shows the MOD values associated with limiting PO_2 from 1.3 to 1.6 atmospheres, and FO_2 ranging from 21 to 36 percent.

You should pay closest attention to the values for PO_2 of 1.3 and 1.4 atmospheres, as they offer the greater safety margin.

Begin by looking at the 32-percent column. The data here show that by using a mixture no richer than EAN32, you can dive as deep as the recommended depth limit for recreational diving of 100 feet/30 metres, and still not exceed a limiting PO_2 of 1.3 atmospheres. Even if you exceed this depth by 10 feet/3 metres, you will not exceed a limiting PO_2 of 1.4 atmospheres. In contrast, EANx mixtures with FO_2 greater than 32 percent do not afford quite as much of a safety margin.

$$\text{FEET} \quad MOD = \left[33 \times \left(\frac{(PO_2)}{(FO_2)} \right) \right] - 33$$

$$\text{METRES} \quad MOD = \left[10 \times \left(\frac{(PO_2)}{(FO_2)} \right) \right] - 10$$

Maximum operating depth (MOD) formulas. Use the top formula for imperial values; the bottom for metric values.

A simple formula for calculating MODs appears to the left using the information on determining MOD for a specific dive as just described. It is generally easier to obtain MOD information by consulting a table.

Analyzing and marking cylinders with MOD information is discussed extensively in the next section.

Limiting total O_2 exposure to safe, CNS "clock" values. Your exposure to elevated PO_2 must not only stay within safer levels (1.4 atmospheres or less), they must also not exceed safe time limits.

The table to the left shows the exposure time limits published by the USA's National Oceanic and Atmospheric Administration (NOAA) for working divers. These are the time limits most widely used in recreational nitrox diving.

As you can see by examining this table, the time limits for a limiting PO_2 of 1.4 atmospheres is 150 minutes for a single dive, and 180 minutes for any 24-hour period. For recreational divers, remaining within these time limits should be easy. The typical recreational diver makes no more than two or three dives a day, averaging no more than 40-60 minutes each.

NOAA Exposure Time Limits for Working Divers

Partial Pressure of Oxygen (PO_2)	Maximum Exposure Time in Minutes	
	Single Dive Limit	24-Hour Limit
0.6	720	720
0.7	570	570
0.8	450	450
0.9	360	360
1.0	300	300
1.1	240	270
1.2	210	240
1.3	180	210
1.4	150	180
1.5	120	180
1.6	45	150

NOAA Exposure Time Limits.

What this means is that, so long as you remain within a limiting PO₂ of 1.4 atmospheres, and keep your accumulated actual bottom time for any 24-hour period well within the three hours allowed, there is simply no need to worry about exceeding the limits. This covers the vast majority of recreational dives.

This method is not only simple and easy to use, it helps minimize the possibility of mathematical error, as would be common in more complex methods of tracking O_2 exposure. For this reason, SSI strongly recommends that recreational nitrox dives not only remain within a limiting PO₂ of 1.4 atmospheres, but also keep accumulated total bottom time for any 24-hour period well within 180 minutes.

Much remains to be discovered regarding the exact causes of CNS oxygen toxicity. Susceptibility to oxygen toxicity may vary from individual to individual and from day to day. Staying within a particular limiting PO₂ and taking additional precautions may still not prevent you from suffering CNS oxygen toxicity. Use extreme caution whenever you expose yourself to elevated partial pressures of oxygen (PO₂).

Now that you better understand how breathing nitrox affects your body, it's time to address its impact on your equipment. This is what we will discuss in Section 3.

Section 2 Review Questions

1. Equivalent Air Depth (EAD) is the best way to compare the
   _____ _____ _____ found in nitrox with that
   found in _____ .

2. The risk of CNS oxygen toxicity becomes more substantial above a
   PO_2 of _____ _____.

3. If you remain within the generally recommended recreational depth limit
   of _____ feet/_____ metres of the surface you will have an extra
   _____ feet/_____ metres safety margin before you exceed a PO_2 of
   _____ _____.

4. The threshold for CNS oxygen toxicity appears to be _____
   _____.

5. Nitrox contains a _____ _____ of nitrogen in
   comparison to air.

6. While oxygen can be toxic to all body tissues, its most noticeable and
   immediate effects take place in the _____ and _____
   _____ _____.

7. It is important to realize that one cannot determine precisely from
   _____ whether they were due to _____
   _____ or some other factor.

8. C + VENT + ID — The symptoms of CNS oxygen toxicity include:
   1. _____
   2. _____
   3. _____
   4. _____
   5. _____
   6. _____
   7. _____

9. If you see your buddy or another diver begin to _____ , hold the diver in place until the convulsions cease, then begin a slow, _____ _____ .

10. In terms of susceptibility to oxygen toxicity, the _____ _____ among individuals, or from one day to the next, may be as great as _____ .

11. Using the Maximum Operating Depth (MOD) table and a recommended limiting PO$_2$ of 1.4, the maximum depth for EAN32 is _____ .

12. Using the Maximum Operating Depth (MOD) table and a recommended limiting PO$_2$ of 1.4, the maximum depth for EAN36 is _____ feet or _____ metres.

2

Your
Total Diving
System and
Nitrox

Section 3 Objectives
After completing this section you will be able to:

◆ Understand how nitrox impacts your Total Diving System,

◆ Determine if your Total Diving System components can be used with nitrox,

◆ Analyze the nitrox content of a scuba cylinder.

The human body was not designed for exposure to elevated partial pressures of oxygen; nevertheless, it has proven surprisingly adaptable. Similarly, most dive equipment was not originally designed for use with nitrox. Fortunately, much of this equipment can be used in conjunction with EANx with little or no modification.

In this section, we examine the considerations involved in using Air Delivery Systems and other items for nitrox diving. You'll learn about the potential problems nitrox may present, and about steps you may need to follow when using your equipment with nitrox.

But first we will deal with the most important skill you need to master during and after your Enriched Air Nitrox Program.

Analyzing Nitrox Cylinder Content

Among the great ironies of learning to use nitrox is the fact that there are no special skills required to actually dive EANx. Once you are under water, a nitrox dive is much like any other. The truly critical skills in nitrox diving involve dive planning and equipment use. Among the most crucial of these skills is the ability to correctly analyze cylinder FO_2 content.

Because of the risks of both CNS oxygen toxicity and decompression sickness, it is vital you personally confirm the oxygen concentration present in every cylinder you dive.

Signing the fill station log.

Protocols for Dispensing Nitrox

When you have a nitrox cylinder filled, or obtain a cylinder from a dive center's rental department, there are certain procedures that the facility will likely have you follow. The facility will most likely either ask you to personally analyze the cylinder's FO_2 content, or witness the analysis as it is performed by one of their staff members. The facility will also most likely have you complete and sign a fill station log, acknowledging both the FO_2 and MOD for the cylinder you are obtaining.

Once you leave the fill station, it is important you maintain control over the cylinder until using it. Otherwise, there is no guarantee the cylinder was not accidentally switched with one similar in appearance, but different in content, or that it has been used or re-filled without your knowledge.

Nitrox filling station.

If you have not been able to maintain personal control over the nitrox cylinder you plan to use, do not assume its contents decal necessarily reflects what is now in the cylinder. Re-analyze the contents before using it.

When you return the cylinder to your SSI Dive Center, or bring a personal nitrox cylinder in for re-filling, the facility will most likely want to know what's inside, both in terms of pressure and FO_2. If the cylinder contents tag no longer accurately reflects the FO_2 of the gas inside the cylinder (a situation that might exist if you had the cylinder refilled with air following the first dive), you should re-analyze its contents so that you can accurately report this information to the fill station operator or blender. Although current standards of practice dictate that the fill station is to do this as well, you can help facilitate the process by telling the staff what to expect prior to refilling the cylinder.

Be aware that whether using your own nitrox cylinder or renting one from an SSI Dive Center, Resort or Charter Operator, the blending facility may have some very specific requirements as to if and how you can have the cylinder re-filled prior to returning it to them. If using rental nitrox cylinders, the facility may simply ask that you not re-fill the cylinders before returning them.

If you are using your own nitrox cylinders that have been O_2 cleaned and O_2 service rated, the facility may ask you to attest to the fact that you have maintained this rating by only allowing the cylinder to be filled with oxygen-compatible air.

If there is any doubt as to whether your cylinder has maintained its O_2 service rating, the facility may require that it undergo another O_2 cleaning prior to filling it.

In general, it's best to remember that dive operators typically prefer you not re-fill dedicated EAN*x* cylinders with anything but nitrox.

The Need to Analyze

Throughout the discussion of nitrox dispensing protocols, one thing should have become apparent. As a nitrox diver, you need to be able to correctly analyze cylinder content, both at the blending station and in the field. This means that you must either own, or have ready access to an oxygen analyzer and flow meter—and you must know how to use this equipment properly.

Do not use any nitrox mixture unless you have either personally analyzed, or witnessed the analysis of its FO_2 content. If you are not certain that the contents tag accurately reflects the cylinder's current FO_2, and the MOD for that FO_2, re-analyze the cylinder. Failure to do so may result in either decompression sickness or CNS oxygen toxicity—which in turn, may lead to serious personal injury or death.

In the balance of Section 3, we will cover the basic procedures needed to analyze cylinder content. As part of your nitrox diver training, you will practice these procedures under the direct supervision of your SSI Instructor.

O_2 Analysis Hardware

To properly analyze cylinder O_2 content, you will need an O_2 analyzer, a flow meter and whatever hardware is required to connect them to the nitrox cylinder you will be analyzing. You will also need a gas source containing either pure oxygen, air or a nitrox mixture whose fraction of oxygen has been established unequivocally to calibrate your O_2 analyzer prior to its use.

The photo at left depicts a typical O_2 analyzer. Any analyzer used for nitrox diving must be accurate to within one percent.

Oxygen analyzer.

Your analyzer unit will come with an oxygen sensor. This may be built in, or be connected to the analyzer unit by means of an electrical cord. In addition to these items, you will need either an oxygen regulator or fixed-rate flow meter to transfer the gas being analyzed to the O_2 sensor at a controlled rate.

The graphic below depicts one possible set-up for analyzing cylinder contents. In this illustration, a normal scuba first-stage regulator connects the cylinder to a fixed-rate flow meter by means of a standard, low-pressure inflation hose. Another common set-up uses the same sort of oxygen regulator as is found in oxygen resuscitation or treatment kits. However, you will have to use special hardware to adapt this regulator for use with standard scuba cylinder valves. The regulator or flow meter connects to the O_2 sensor, which in turn connects to the O_2 analyzer.

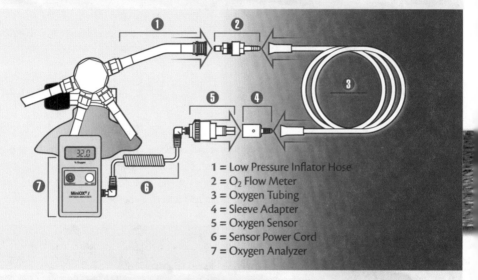

1 = Low Pressure Inflator Hose
2 = O_2 Flow Meter
3 = Oxygen Tubing
4 = Sleeve Adapter
5 = Oxygen Sensor
6 = Sensor Power Cord
7 = Oxygen Analyzer

An analysis set-up consisting of a second-stage regulator, fixed-rate flow meter, an O_2 sensor and analyzer.

The O_2 sensor is among the most critical links in this chain. It typically contains a volatile chemical that will deteriorate over time. This means you will most likely have to replace the sensor periodically. You can prolong sensor life by storing it in a sealed plastic bag between uses.

O_2 sensors are also typically sensitive to changes in atmospheric pressure and moisture. This is why you must calibrate your analyzer each time you use it. If you did not, you would discover

O_2 Sensor Sensitivity

Your O_2 sensor may be sensitive to changes in temperature. If it is cold, you should allow it to warm to ambient temperature before using it.

that each time you analyzed the same gas you would get a slightly different reading.

The instructions accompanying some analyzers may say that you are to calibrate them against a source containing pure oxygen. Since the gas you will be analyzing is closer in FO_2 content to air, it may make sense to calibrate the unit against a pure air source, or against another gas source (such as the store's premixed nitrox supply) whose oxygen concentration has been established unequivocally. Ask your SSI Dive Center if this is permissible.

Note: O_2 analyzers designed for use by nitrox divers almost always specify that you are to calibrate them against air.

Analysis Procedures

Oxygen analyzer calibration.

Here are the general procedures you will follow when analyzing cylinder O_2 content. These procedures may vary slightly depending on the analyzer set-up you use; your SSI Dive Center can help you identify what these differences may be.

1. Begin by connecting your analyzer system to its calibration source, be that a cylinder of pure oxygen, premixed nitrox or air.

2. Turn the calibration source on. If using an oxygen regulator, adjust the flow rate to that specified by the analyzer manufacturer. Fixed rate meters generally restrict gas flow to a rate of approximately two litres per minute. This is an acceptable rate for most analyzers.

3. Once gas is flowing, and has had the opportunity to displace the air previously in the line, adjust the calibration dial so that it reads either 100.0 percent for oxygen, 20.9 percent for air or the correct percentage for another calibration source, if used. (The calibration dial may be very sensitive; getting the setting within ± 0.1 percent of the target is generally considered adequate.)

4. Allow the calibration gas to flow for at least 30 seconds. Make certain there are no substantial variations in reading during this time. (If you will be analyzing several cylinders in succession, you only need to calibrate your analyzer once.)

5. Disconnect the analyzer set-up from the calibration source. Reconnect it to the cylinder you will be analyzing.

6. Allow gas to flow until the analyzer reading stabilizes. Continue to allow gas to flow for another 30 seconds to ensure this reading remains constant.

7. Disconnect and store your analyzer in a safe place. Remember to seal the O$_2$ sensor in a plastic bag.

In some areas, local regulations or standards of practice dictate that O$_2$ analysis be done by using two analyzers in parallel. Hence, each analyzer helps confirm the accuracy of the other.

Occasionally, you may see divers trying to analyze gas by holding the O_2 sensor in the general vicinity of the valve orifice. This is called a "sniff" test, and it is not an accurate way to analyze cylinder content. It is important you calibrate your analyzer each time you use it — and to do so in a sealed system with the calibration gas at the same flow rate and moisture content as the gas you will be analyzing.

How Nitrox Use Impacts Your Total Diving System

The only pieces of dive equipment with which we need to concern ourselves in regard to nitrox are those that come into direct contact with the gas. These items include the Air Delivery System (cylinder, first- and second-stage regulators) and any attached components. The chief concerns regarding these items are increased oxidation and the risk of fire or explosion.

Increased Oxidation and Wear

The o-rings, seals and other components used in many pieces of scuba equipment are subject to oxidation. Over time, substances such as neoprene combine with oxygen and deteriorate. When used with air, this oxidation takes place at an anticipated rate. Before this deterioration reaches the point at which it causes problems, it can be dealt with through normal preventive maintenance.

Oxidation

Because nitrox contains substantially more oxygen than air does, use of some equipment items with nitrox may cause oxidation to take place at a much faster rate than originally anticipated.

The Risk of Fire or Explosion

Although the air normally used to fill scuba cylinders is safe for human consumption, it is not absolutely pure. It contains traces of hydrocarbons and other contaminants. Over time, these can build up on the internal surfaces of an Air Delivery System.

$O_2 =$

Ordinarily, this build-up would not cause any problems. However, when exposed to pure oxygen, or gas mixtures with unusually high FO_2, these contaminants can cause spontaneous combustion, resulting in potentially lethal fires or explosions.

Additionally, the silicone lubricant normally used to service scuba first- and second-stage regulators and valves, as well as the materials used in some o-rings and seals, are also flammable when exposed to high concentrations of oxygen under pressure.

Using Standard Scuba Equipment with Nitrox

Because of the problems nitrox may cause to some items of equipment, before using EAN*x* with any equipment you presently own or plan to acquire, you must first determine whether:

♦ The equipment can be used with nitrox without any special preparation or modifications.

♦ There are procedures or modifications you must perform before allowing a particular equipment item to come into contact with EAN*x*.

♦ The equipment can simply never be used with anything but air.

The 40 Percent Rule

Two United States government agencies have done a substantial portion of the pioneering work with nitrox and established the standards of practice for EAN*x* used throughout much of the world. These are the National Oceanic and Atmospheric Administration (NOAA) and the United States Navy. Both agencies, as well as the United States Coast Guard, operate under what many call the

What is the 40 Percent Rule?

Simply stated, when any equipment item is exposed to gas mixtures with FO_2 of no more than 40 percent, no special preparation, modification or maintenance procedures are required. This covers virtually all equipment items except scuba cylinders and valves.

40 percent rule. This rule has become the standard of practice throughout much of the world.

If scuba cylinders and valves will be exposed to pure oxygen, or enriched air mixtures of more than 40 percent, then they must first be O_2 clean and O_2 service rated.

Although the 40 percent rule is widely followed, its acceptance is not universal. In some instances, local laws or regulations stipulate that all equipment exposed to gases with oxygen concentrations greater than air be oxygen clean and oxygen service rated or a completely different Total Diving System used specifically for higher concentrations of Oxygen.

Some equipment manufacturers state that use of their equipment with anything other than air will void the warranty.

Alternately, manufacturers may specify special preparation and maintenance procedures that divers and service facilities must follow to use their equipment with nitrox. Increasingly, manufacturers are marketing special lines of Air Delivery Systems, instruments, valves and cylinders for use with nitrox.

What Rules Should You Follow?

As far as using any dive equipment you presently own or plan to acquire with nitrox, you must comply with local laws, regulations and standards of practice among dive operators. In some areas, these will require that any component of the Total Diving System that comes in contact with gases whose oxygen concentration is greater than that of air, must first be O_2 clean and O_2 service rated (procedures we cover shortly).

You must follow the manufacturer's specifications for use of your dive equipment. Rather than try to discern what these are on your own, your better choice is to consult your local SSI Dive Center. Your dive center can make specific recommendations regarding possible modification of your present equipment, and suggestions for new equipment you may want or need to acquire.

If a piece of equipment is not covered by local laws, regulations or standards of practice, or by specific manufacturer recommendations or requirements, you may apply the 40 percent rule to determine whether it must be O_2 clean and O_2 service rated to be used in conjunction with nitrox.

The SSI Equipment Service Program

Your SSI Dive Center may offer the SSI Equipment Service Program, a complete maintenance program designed to keep the components of your Total Diving System performing to the best of their potential. Below is an explanation of each of the services that make up the SSI Equipment Service Program.

Air Delivery System Protection

Regulators are totally disassembled and cleaned in a special cleaning solution. High-pressure and low-pressure seats are replaced along with all dynamic o-rings, exhaust valves, and high pressure filters. Performance tests are conducted to manufacturer warranty specifications.

Nitrox Air Delivery System Protection

This is the same as Air Delivery System Protection, but is performed on nitrox equipment. A green nitrox hose sleeve is used to mark your nitrox Air Delivery System rather than a yellow hose sleeve.

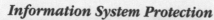

Information System Protection

Submersible pressure gauges, depth gauges, pressure activated dive timers, and dive computers are checked for accuracy in a pressure vessel, and the indicated readings versus true readings are noted.

Buoyancy Control System Protection

Buoyancy compensators are inspected for buckle strap tension and bladder seam integrity. Inflator mechanisms are disassembled, cleaned and rebuilt, the inner bladder rinsed with BC conditioner and over-pressure release valves are cleaned and tested for proper operation, all to manufacturer warranty specifications.

Visual Inspection Protection (and Visual Plus®)

Annually, cylinders are inspected internally and externally for rust and corrosion to the standards of DOT and CGA. It's suggested that aluminum cylinders be tested with Visual Plus to ensure the integrity and strength of the neck and threads.

Exposure System Protection

Services are available for exposure suits (wet and dry). Minor repairs are done in-house and alterations are done with the original manufacturer.

When you have your equipment serviced or repaired, take along your SSI Total DiveLog so the technician can record the service. This will be valuable should you decide to upgrade your equipment someday.

Nitrox and Scuba Cylinders

Depending on the method used to fill them, there are special procedures that may apply to scuba cylinders that are not necessarily applicable to other equipment with which nitrox comes in contact. Also, there are special markings that need to be applied to any cylinder that may contain nitrox.

Note: For more information on The Significance of Blending Methods, What do the Terms "O_2 Clean" and "O_2 Service Rated" mean and The Significance of Oxygen-Compatible Air please check the Appendix of this manual.

Nitrox Cylinder Markings

Any scuba cylinder that may contain gases other than air must be labeled as such. Were a diver to use an unmarked cylinder containing nitrox, mistakenly thinking it was air, he or she would risk unanticipated CNS oxygen toxicity. Likewise, were a nitrox diver to use a cylinder containing air, mistakenly thinking it was EAN*x*, he or she might increase his or her risk of decompression sickness.

The exact standards for marking nitrox cylinders may vary, depending on where you live or dive. What we will cover in this section are the standards most widely used throughout the world.

Enriched Air Nitrox

1.0 in/25mm Yellow

4.0 in/10cm Green

1.0 in/25mm Yellow

Sufficient length to encircle cylinder without obscuring any wording

The graphic above depicts the most widely used marking scheme for nitrox cylinders. The colors used are green and yellow. Green and yellow have established themselves as a common color code for nitrox, and also appear on many nitrox compatible first- and second-stage regulators, valves and dive computers. The wording on the 4 inch/10 cm encircling band may be Nitrox, Enriched Air or Enriched Air Nitrox.

It is important to understand what these or similar markings do and do not mean. The only thing you can really count on is that a cylinder bearing nitrox markings may contain EAN*x* at an undetermined FO_2. Then again, it is entirely possible that such a cylinder has been refilled largely with air. In addition, the presence of basic nitrox markings does not indicate whether a cylinder is O_2 clean or O_2 service rated. This must be indicated by a separate decal.

ENRICHED·AIR NITROX
READ WARNING LABEL • ANALYZE BEFORE USING

⚠ WARNING

■ Enriched Air Nitrox (EANx) diving entails additional risks not present when diving air, including the risk of Central Nervous System (CNS) oxygen toxicity, which can lead to loss of consciousness underwater, resulting in serious personal injury or death. Obtain special training and certification from a qualified instructor before diving nitrox.

■ The presence of this decal, or any other decal or marking tag indicating cylinder contents, does not necessarily guarantee that this cylinder contains Enriched Air Nitrox, or nitrox at any given Fraction of Oxygen (FO_2). Unless you have personally analyzed, or witnessed the analysis of the contents of this cylinder, and are absolutely certain it has not been used or re-filled since that time, always analyze and verify its contents before breathing the gas it contains.

■ Do not assume that the presence of this decal indicates that this cylinder is oxygen clean or oxygen service rated. Look for a separate decal indicating whether this cylinder may be filled with gases whose FO_2 is greater than 40 percent.

■ Use dive tables and other planning tools conservatively and correctly. Be aware, however, that even if you do so, decompression sickness or CNS oxygen toxicity may still occur.

SSI's recommended nitrox cylinder markings. The graphic at left is a full-size reproduction of the warning label found on the encircling band.

The graphic above depicts SSI's recommended nitrox cylinder decal. It spells out more clearly what the encircling band does and does not mean. It also provides some basic warnings regarding nitrox use. Most importantly, it reminds divers of the vital importance of personally analyzing, or witnessing the analysis of the FO_2 level of the gas contained in the cylinder prior to using it.

In addition to the encircling band, there are at least two other marking devices every nitrox cylinder should have.

The graphic at lower left depicts decals that show whether a cylinder has been O_2 cleaned and O_2 service rated. This information may also be incorporated into the cylinder's visual inspection decal. If it is not, a separate visual inspection decal is required.

O₂ YES

This cylinder has been oxygen cleaned and oxygen service rated

On the date appearing below, this cylinder was cleaned and serviced in accordance with prevailing standards of practice for oxygen service. As long as this cylinder has been *filled solely with oxygen compatible air* since that time, it may be used for in-cylinder, partial-pressure blending of Enriched Air Nitrox (EANx).

Service Date:

Serviced By:

Facility:

SSI. SCUBA SCHOOLS INTERNATIONAL

Decal indicating whether a cylinder has been O_2 cleaned and O_2 service rated.

The photo, right, depicts a typical cylinder contents tag or decal. It is important that every nitrox cylinder be clearly labeled as to its FO_2 content and the Maximum Operating Depth (MOD) for that FO_2. It should also be clear who analyzed the cylinder, and when they did so.

Ideally, the MOD markings should also indicate what limiting PO_2 value they are for. Some nitrox blenders still provide MOD information based on a limiting PO_2 of 1.6 atmospheres. This can be misleading when you are trying to stay within more conservative PO_2 of 1.3 or 1.4 atmospheres.

You should always check the FO_2 and MOD contents markings against MOD tables, such as those appearing in Sections 2. If the MOD appearing on the contents tag reflects a limiting PO_2 greater than 1.4 atmospheres, disregard it and use an MOD that reflects a more conservative limiting PO_2 of no more than 1.4 atmospheres.

Summary

Congratulations!

You Have Completed the Academic Portion of SSI's Enriched Air Nitrox Diver 32.

To dive EAN32, you will have to pass a final performance review.

Section 3 Review Questions

1. It is important that every nitrox cylinder be clearly labeled as to its _____ and the _____ _____ _____ (_____) for that FO_2. It should also be clear _____ _____ the cylinder, and when they did so.

2. Because of the risks of both CNS oxygen toxicity and decompression sickness, it is vital you _____ _____ the _____ _____ present in every cylinder you dive.

3. Begin by connecting your analyzer system to its calibration source, be that a _____ _____ _____ _____, _____ _____ or _____.

4. Allow the calibration gas to flow for at least _____ seconds.

5. Once you _____ the fill station, it is important you _____ _____ over the cylinder until using it.

6. In some areas, local _____ or _____ dictate that O_2 analysis be done by using two analyzers in parallel.

7. If _____ _____ and _____ will be ex posed to pure oxygen, or enriched air mixtures of _____ _____ _____ percent, then they must first be O_2 clean and O_2 service rated.

8. You must follow the _____ _____ for use of your dive equipment.

9. You should always check the _____ and _____

contents markings against MOD tables, such as those appearing in

Section 2.

10. Any _____ that may contain \ other than

_____ must be labeled as such.

Planning Your Nitrox Dives

In Section 3, we pointed out that there are no special skills involved in actually diving nitrox except analyzing cylinder content. A very important skill is learning how to prepare for and plan nitrox dives.

Section 4 Objectives
After completing this section you will be able to:

◆ Use a nitrox-programmable computer for nitrox dive planning,

◆ Manage your exposure to oxygen by using nitrox-programmable computers,

◆ Handle your exposure to nitrogen using nitrox-programmable computers,

◆ Perform nitrox dive planning and the decision-making process.

Much of the planning that takes place when diving air involves managing your exposure to nitrogen.

Managing your exposure to nitrogen remains an important part of planning nitrox dives—with a few possible changes.

Although diving nitrox reduces your exposure to nitrogen, it does not eliminate it. Even though you use one or more of the accepted methods for planning nitrox dives correctly, you may still suffer decompression sickness.

The way in which planning nitrox dives differs most from planning air dives is that, when diving EANx, you must also manage your exposure to oxygen. Fortunately, for nitrox divers who remain within normal recreational diving limits, this can be a very simple and straight forward procedure.

A key factor in deciding which method to use is whether your primary goal in diving nitrox is to achieve more dive time or to ensure a greater safety margin. At the end of Section 4,

you will find a flow-chart-type analysis that shows exactly how this decision-making process might take place.

Just like technology has entered our daily lives with iPhones and Laptops, so have dive computers become mainstream in recreational diving. For this reason, SSI has chosen to focus on the use of nitrox-programmable computers for this program. You can still learn all about nitrox dive tables by watching Section 4 of the Enriched Air Nitrox DVD and turning to the Appendix of this manual. Note: Teaching the use of nitrox tables is at the Instructor's discretion.

Be aware that the discussion that follows assumes you are already proficient in applying the decompression theory from your entry level training. If you need to review this topic with your SSI Instructor, do so before reading further.

Using Nitrox-Programmable Dive Computers

A number of manufacturers offer dive computers that can be programmed for nitrox. One benefit of nitrox-programmable computers is that they allow nitrox divers to enjoy the maximum possible dive time. If you were to program such a computer for an FO_2 of, say, 32 percent, the computer would give you the longer bottom times, shorter surface intervals and longer repetitive dives normally associated with EAN32.

Most nitrox-programmable dive computers not only track a diver's exposure to nitrogen, they also track the diver's exposure to oxygen.

Using computers is a more convenient way to dive and generally problems are caused from diver error. We recommend the SSI Computer Diving Specialty to teach you everything you need to know about your computer.

The graphic, to the left, shows such a computer. The computer's display contains a bar graph showing where the user stands in terms of his or her total allowable oxygen "dose." This information enables a diver to manage his or her total exposure to both nitrogen and oxygen. Many experts feel this ability may be the single greatest benefit of using nitrox-programmable dive computers.

Oxygen Exposure Bar Graph

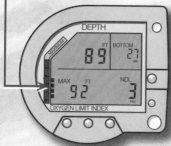

Some nitrox-programmable dive computers also track a diver's exposure to oxygen.

Nitrox-programmable dive computers make diving easy. They track both nitrogen and oxygen exposure.

Dive computers are great for planning and executing dives. They record all pertinent information to keep you safe and confident. Here are a few guidelines to follow:

1. Do not share a dive computer

2. Check the dive computer battery before diving

3. Observe and adhere to dive computer warnings
   ♦ Ascent rates
   ♦ Decompression limits
   ♦ Nitrogen exposure
   ♦ Oxygen exposure

4. Dive conservatively

5. Plan your dive, dive your plan

6. Have a contingency plan, if your computer fails

7. If you experience a computer failure:
   ♦ Signal your buddy that you need to start your ascent
   ♦ Ascend with your buddy while he/she monitors your ascent on their computer
   ♦ Perform a longer than normal safety stop if air supply permits as an added precaution
   ♦ Do not enter the water again for at least 24 hours and watch for the signs of Decompression Sickness (DCS)

Managing Exposure to Oxygen

In Section 2, we addressed what is perhaps the single most important aspect of managing your exposure to oxygen. That is, controlling the intensity of that exposure by determining a Maximum Operating Depth (MOD), based on a limiting PO_2 of 1.4 atmospheres or less.

In addition to controlling the intensity of your exposure to oxygen, you must also control the length of that exposure. Combined, these two factors determine your total oxygen "dose." This is what we will address over the next several pages.

Understanding the Oxygen "Dose"

Each time you dive, your body is exposed to the effects of oxygen. The easiest way to understand the cumulative effects of oxygen is to compare it to taking a prescription drug. Your doctor may tell you to take 100 units of a particular drug every day. He or she may tell you to take four 25 unit pills, or two 50 unit pills. Either way, the dose is the same. They may even tell you to never take more than 75 units in a single dose because it could be harmful to your health.

As divers, we are given similar instructions on how we "take" oxygen. For example, when the PO_2 is 1.4, our limit is 180 minutes in a 24 hour period. We could reach that limit by making six, 30 minute dives or by making two 90 minute dives. We could even get the same dose by making two, 20 minute dives plus two 70 minute dives. In all of these examples, the total exposure adds up to the daily limit of 180 minutes.

CNS "Clock" Values

The time it takes for a diver to accumulate a full "dose" (100%) of oxygen depends on the PO_2. Diving where the PO_2 values are high can be compared to taking a strong pill and where PO_2 values are small can be compared to taking a weak pill.

When tracking oxygen the exposure, we substitute the term "clock" in place of "dose". When you have received the maximum "dose," you are said to have used 100% (the limit) of your "clock." When diving where PO_2 values are high, you reach the "clock" limit faster. When the PO_2 values are small, you can dive longer before you reach the "clock" limit.

On each dive you determine the percentage of the "clock" limit that you received. When making multiple dives, you add the percentages together and avoid exceeding 100%.

Simplified Approaches to Managing Oxygen Exposure

The simplest way to manage your exposure to oxygen is to dive with a computer that tracks your O_2 exposure. Analyze your gas, set the FO_2 (or percent) value in your computer, and observe any limits or warnings it displays. This method also provides all of the other benefits you gain from diving with a computer which include; tracking nitrogen absorption, maximizing your bottom time, and the ability to accurately monitor your ascent rate.

An alternative, simple approach to managing your exposure to oxygen is for you to remain within the maximum PO_2 of 1.4 atmospheres and make certain that your total bottom time for all dives on a 24-hour period does not exceed 180 minutes (100% of your daily clock). You must also make certain that you do not "overdose" by exceeding 150 minutes on any single dive within the day.

This method will work for a majority of dive days. At first, a daily limit of 180 minutes may seem sufficient. Consider however, that many liveaboards and some resorts provide the opportunity to dive four to five hours a day. It is important in these situations to understand how the oxygen "dose" changes when the PO_2 is decreased, and to understand the technique we use to add together the oxygen exposure from several dives.

What this means is that, so long as you remain within a limiting PO_2 of 1.4 atmospheres, and keep your accumulated actual bottom time for any 24-hour period well within the three hours allowed, there is simply no need to worry about exceeding the limits. This covers the vast majority of recreational dives. This method is not only simple and easy to use, it helps minimize the possibility of mathematical error, as would be common in more complex methods of tracking O_2 exposure. For this reason, SSI strongly recommends that recreational nitrox dives not only remain within a limiting PO_2 of 1.4 atmospheres, but also keep accumulated total bottom time for any 24-hour period well within 180 minutes.

Tracking CNS "Clock" Values

If you make multiple nitrox dives where the total bottom time in a 24-hour period exceeds 180 minutes, or the PO_2 on any of your dives exceeds 1.4, you must track your "clock" values. A nitrox computer is still the best option, but with a little practice you can become proficient in tracking the values yourself.

CNS "CLOCK" EXPOSURE TIME TABLE — SSI

Partial Pressure of Oxygen (PO₂)	Maximum Exposure Time in Minutes — Single Dive Limit	24-Hour Limit	— Actual Bottom Time in Minutes — 5	10	15	20	25	30	35	40	45	50	55	60
0.6	720	720	1%	1%	2%	3%	3%	4%	5%	6%	6%	7%	8%	8%
0.7	570	570	1%	2%	3%	4%	4%	5%	6%	7%	8%	9%	10%	11%
0.8	450	450	1%	2%	3%	4%	6%	7%	8%	9%	10%	11%	12%	13%
0.9	360	360	1%	3%	4%	6%	7%	8%	10%	11%	13%	14%	15%	17%
1.0	300	300	2%	3%	5%	7%	8%	10%	12%	13%	15%	17%	18%	20%
1.1	240	270	2%	4%	6%	8%/7%	10%/9%	13%/11%	15%/13%	17%/15%	19%/17%	21%/19%	23%/20%	25%/22%
1.2	210	240	2%	5%/4%	7%/6%	10%/8%	12%/10%	14%/13%	17%/15%	19%/17%	21%/19%	24%/21%	26%/23%	29%/25%
1.3	180	210	3%/2%	6%/5%	8%/7%	11%/10%	14%/12%	17%/14%	19%/17%	22%/19%	25%/21%	28%/24%	31%/26%	33%/29%
1.4	150	180	3%	7%/6%	10%/8%	13%/11%	17%/14%	20%/17%	23%/19%	27%/22%	30%/25%	33%/28%	37%/31%	40%/33%
1.5	120	180	4%/3%	8%/6%	13%/8%	17%/11%	21%/14%	25%/17%	29%/19%	33%/22%	38%/25%	42%/28%	46%/31%	50%/33%
1.6	45	150	11%/3%	22%/7%	33%/10%	44%/13%	56%/17%	67%/20%	78%/23%	89%/27%	100%/30%	111%/33%	122%/37%	133%/40%

See reverse side for important warnings • Consult SSI NITROX DIVER MANUAL for detailed instructions on use of this table.

© 1996 CONCEPT SYSTEMS, INC. • Reorder Nº ????EAN (FEET) –or– 2506M-EAN (METRES)

CNS "Clock" Exposure Time Table.

CNS "CLOCK"

Partial Pressure of Oxygen (PO₂)	Maximum Exposure Time in Minutes — Single Dive Limit	24-Hour Limit
0 6	720	720
0 7	570	570
0 8	450	450
0 9	360	360
1 0	300	300
1 1	240	270
1 2	210	240
1.3	180	210
1.4	(150)	(180)
1.5	120	180

For each dive you make, determine the maximum PO_2 that you will experience during the dive. Find this PO_2 value in the left-hand column and follow its row across to the next column entitled "Clock Limits". There you will find listed the dive "clock" limit (green) and the 24-hour "clock" limit (yellow).

As an example, let's use the PO_2 value that you are familiar with. Find 1.4 in the left-hand column. In the next column, you find 150 minutes in green. This represents the maximum dive time ("clock" value) for any one single dive during the day. To the right in yellow, you find 180 minutes. This is the maximum "clock" value when you add the bottom times of all the dives in a 24-hour period together.

The smallest PO₂ value on the SSI CNS "Clock" Exposure Time Table is 0.6. A conservative approach to tracking oxygen exposure is to treat dives with a PO₂ of 0.5 and less as if they equal to 0.6.

Now let's look at an example of how we use this chart to track the oxygen exposure when we make two dives and the PO₂ is not the same.

You plan to make a dive to 86 feet/26 metres while breathing EAN32. First, you would consult the computer or Combined Air/EANx Dive Tables to determine how long you can dive. Let's assume the dive time is 40 minutes. Your computer or table for the corresponding PO₂ for that depth would be 1.16.

To track the oxygen exposure for the dive above, you round the 1.16 to a PO₂ of 1.2 and find that value in the left-hand column of the SSI CNS "Clock" Exposure Time Table. Follow the 1.2 PO₂ row to the right until it falls under the "Actual Bottom Time In Minutes" column corresponding to the dive time of 40 minutes. There you find 19% in green and 17% in yellow. The 19% value represents how close you came to using up your single dive "clock" limit. In this case, a relatively small percentage was used. The 17% value represents the amount of your daily, 24-hour "clock" limit (dose) that you used. On dive days, be certain to record these "clock" values in your SSI Logbook as they will be needed later.

On our first dive of the day, you have used 17% of the daily "clock" value. This means that you could make at least four more dives like this one within the 24-hour period. This, however, is highly unlikely as the process of nitrogen absorption and elimination will

CNS "CLOCK" EXPOSURE TIME TABL

Partial Pressure of Oxygen (PO₂)	Maximum Exposure Time in Minutes		— Actual Bottom Time in Mi							
	Single Dive Limit	24-Hour Limit	5	10	15	20	25	30	35	40
0.6	720	720	1%	1%	2%	3%	3%	4%	5%	6%
0.7	570	570	1%	2%	3%	4%	4%	5%	6%	7%
0.8	450	450	1%	2%	3%	4%	6%	7%	8%	9%
0.9	360	360	1%	3%	4%	6%	7%	8%	10%	11%
1.0	300	300	2%	3%	5%	7%	8%	10%	12%	13%
1.1	240	270	2%	4%	6%	8% 7%	10% 9%	13% 11%	15% 13%	17% 15%
1.2	210	240	2%	5% 4%	7% 6	8%	10%	14% 13	17% 15	19% 17%

require you to dive more shallow, or for less time, as the day progresses.

Let's assume after a 1:15 surface interval, you are planning a repetitive dive to 57 feet/17 metres, breathing EAN35.

Either your computer or your combined Air/EANx Dive Table will show your PO_2 is approximately 0.98.

You know from experience, and from having previously calculated your SAC rate, that your gas supply will last you about 45 minutes at this depth so that becomes your planned bottom time.

To track the oxygen exposure for this repetitive dive that you are planning, you start by rounding the 0.98 to a PO_2 of 1.0. You find the 1.0 value in the left hand column of the SSI CNS "Clock" Exposure Time Table and follow the row until it intersects the 45-minute column. There you will find 15% in green and 15% in yellow. The percentages are the same because, at this PO_2, the single dive and 24-hour "clock" limits are the same.

CNS "CLOCK" EXPOSURE TIME TABLE

Partial Pressure of Oxygen (PO_2)	Maximum Exposure Time in Minutes		— Actual Bottom Time in Minutes								
	Single Dive Limit	24-Hour Limit	5	10	15	20	25	30	35	40	45
0 6	720	720	1%	1%	2%	3%	3%	4%	5%	6%	6%
0 7	570	570	1%	2%	3%	4%	4%	5%	6%	7%	8%
0 8	450	450	1%	2%	3%	4%	6%	7%	8%	9%	10%
0.9	360	360	1%	3%	4%	6%	7%	8%	10%	11%	13%
1.0	300	300	2%	3%	5%	7%	8%	10%	12%	13%	15%

You can readily see that you have not come close to exceeding the single dive limit and you have picked up an additional 15% to add to your daily limit. To determine your total daily "dose" so far, you add the 24-hour "clock" value from dive one to the 24-hour "clock" value for dive two and determine that you have used 32% (17% + 15%) of your allowed 100%. At this point you have 68% of your daily limit still remaining!

The total of all percentages for all dives within any 24-hour period must not exceed 100%.

You simply repeat this process of utilizing your computer or the Combined Air/EANx Dive Tables to determine dive times and utilizing the SSI CNS "Clock" Exposure Time Table to determine clock values as you make additional dives throughout the day. You may also need to utilize the Equivalent Depths Table in conjunction with your air table if you use a nitrox blend other than EAN32, EAN36, or air.

Note: If you are diving a computer, the use of the CNS Clock Exposure Time Table may not be necessary as computers take into account depth and nitrox percentage when planning and executing your dives.

Other Considerations

Although the NOAA Exposure Time Limits have proven helpful in the real world, you should be aware that the values they give are theoretical. They have not been empirically tested the way the US Navy and other dive tables have been. For this reason, many nitrox divers prefer to exceed no more than 80-90 percent of the NOAA time limits.

NOAA Exposure Time Limit is no more than three hours in one 24-hour period at a PO_2 of 1.4.

The single most important aspect of limiting your exposure to oxygen is keeping within conservative PO_2 levels. This is why, throughout this manual, we've advised you to remain within a limiting PO_2 of 1.4 atmospheres or less. Still, your body will benefit from having time to recover after each exposure. Many nitrox divers like to take at least an hour surface interval between nitrox dives and any other subsequent air dives.

Tracking CNS "Clock" Values

As a recreational nitrox Diver, it is highly unlikely you will even come close to the NOAA limits — especially if you follow SSI's recommendations concerning limiting PO_2 and accumulated actual bottom time. Nevertheless, the possibility exists. How would you deal with it?

This is an area in which having a dive computer that tracks O_2 exposure may be very helpful. Lacking this, you would have to determine how much of your CNS "clock" you used up on each dive you made.

Managing Exposure to Nitrogen

When planning nitrox dives, you can manage your exposure to nitrogen in a variety of ways. Many of these ways can work in combination with others. This enables you to choose the method(s) of dive planning that best fit your individual needs.

The strategies available to nitrox divers for managing exposure to nitrogen include:

◆ Use a nitrox-programmable dive computer.

◆ Use a computer or the SSI Air-Based Dive Tables without modification.

◆ Use equivalent air depths in conjunction with an air-based dive table.

◆ Use the SSI Combined Air/EAN*x* Dive Tables.

Over the next several pages, we will examine each of these methods, not only explaining how you would use them, but also the factors involved in determining whether a particular method meets your individual needs. A key factor in deciding which method to use is whether your primary goal in diving nitrox is to achieve more dive time or to ensure a greater safety margin. At the end of Section 4, you will find a flow-chart-type analysis that shows exactly how this decision-making process might take place.

Using Air Computers or Air-Based Dive Tables with Nitrox

One means of controlling your exposure to nitrogen when diving nitrox, is to simply continue to use the same dive tables or dive computer that you do when diving air. The potential benefits of doing so include:

♦ You greatly simplify the dive-planning process by using the same tools as you do when diving air.

♦ To some degree, you reduce your risk of decompression sickness by basing your dive plans on the assumption your breathing mixture contains more nitrogen than it actually does.

The chief drawback of this approach is that you will not gain increased bottom time, shorter surface intervals or longer repetitive dives, which are among the chief reasons many people dive nitrox in the first place.

Remember that, even though you may use an air-based computer or dive table when diving nitrox, you must still take steps to ensure your exposure to oxygen does not exceed acceptable levels. Failure to do so may result in CNS oxygen toxicity which, in turn, can cause serious personal injury.

Using Equivalent Air Depths

A common way to plan nitrox dives is to use the concept of Equivalent Air Depth (EAD) in conjunction with the same tables divers normally use on air dives. There are a number of ways divers can do this.

EAD is another way of saying, "If you breathe a particular nitrox mixture at this depth, you will expose your body to the same overall level of nitrogen as you would experience when breathing air at this shallower depth." EAD is the primary basis for planning nitrox dives. As an example, an EAN32 dive to 98 feet/29 metres has an EAD of just 80 feet/24 metres. This means we can make such a dive using air-based dive table values for the shallower depth. Equivalent Depth Tables appear and will be covered extensively in the Appendix as well as Formulas for calculating equivalent air depths.

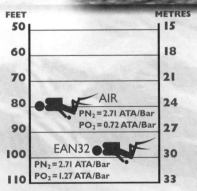

The concept of equivalent air depth.

One approach to using EADs is to work a mathematical formula that will provide the EAD for any combination of depth and FO_2. Two examples of such formulas appear here. However, as the solutions to these equations never vary, it is simply easier to look up this information on a table.

Enriched Air Nitrox Equivalent Air Depth (EAD)

The formula below can be used to find the EAD when actual depth is known.

This formula is of greatest value if the maximum possible depth of a dive is known, and one wanted to use this knowledge to calculate the most precise EAD possible. The variable D represents actual depth in feet or metres.

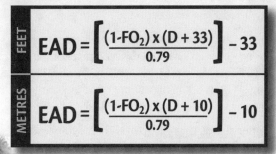

FEET
$$EAD = \left[\frac{(1\text{-}FO_2) \times (D + 33)}{0.79} \right] - 33$$

METRES
$$EAD = \left[\frac{(1\text{-}FO_2) \times (D + 10)}{0.79} \right] - 10$$

**Equivalent air depth (EAD) formulas.
Use the top formula for imperial values;
the bottom for metric values.**

These are the formulas used to generate the SSI Equivalent Depth table.

FEET
$$D = \left[\frac{0.79 \times (EAD + 33)}{(1\text{-}FO_2)} \right] - 33$$

METRES
$$D = \left[\frac{0.79 \times (EAD + 10)}{(1\text{-}FO_2)} \right] - 10$$

**Actual depth formulas. Use the top formula for
imperial values; the bottom for metric values.**

The Nitrox Dive Planning and Decision-Making Process

With so many planning tools and options available, it should be clear that diving nitrox is as much a decision-making process as it is a planning process. The flow chart on page 4-15 outlines just exactly what this decision-making process may entail.

Here is an overview of that process in greater detail.

Define Your Goal

Odds are, you dive nitrox for one of two reasons: Either you wish to maximize dive time, or you want to achieve an even greater margin of safety than diving air within the same depth and time limits would otherwise provide. Which of these goals is more important to you will determine which tools you use to manage your exposure to nitrogen.

If your goal is to maximize safety, you will want to plan your dives using either an air-based dive computer or the SSI Air-Based Dive Tables. However, as mentioned earlier in this section, doing so does not eliminate the need to keep your exposure to oxygen within recommended limits.

On the other hand, if your goal is to maximize dive time, your choice of planning tools will include Nitrox programmable dive computers or a combination of the SSI Tables. As mentioned earlier, many Nitrox dive computers will also help you track and manage your oxygen exposure. For this reason, SSI strongly recommends the use of nitrox programmable dive computers.

What is your primary goal in diving Nitrox?

More dive time
Use a Nitrox-programmable dive computer or the Equivalent Depth conversion table or the combined Air/EANx table to manage exposure to Nitrogen.

Greater safety
Use an air-based computer or dive table to manage exposure to Nitrogen.

Will total Actual Bottom Time in any 24-hour period exceed 180 minutes?

No
Did you exceed a limiting PO₂ of 1.4 atmospheres?

No
No additional planning required; total oxygen dose already within recommended limits.

Yes
Check your Nitrox Computer or use CNS "Clock" Exposure Time Table to ensure total oxygen dose does not exceed recommended limits.

Decision-making process for planning nitrox dives.

Managing Oxygen Exposure

Once you've decided how you will manage your exposure to nitrogen, the next step is to determine how you will track and manage your exposure to oxygen. As just discussed, this should be fairly easy—simply remain within a limiting PO_2 of 1.4 atmospheres and keep total accumulated dive time for any 24-hour period within 180 minutes.

Should you exceed either of these parameters, you have two choices. You can either rely on a nitrox dive computer that tracks both nitrogen and oxygen exposure, or use the SSI CNS "Clock" Exposure Time Table. Still, the best choice of all is not to put yourself in this position in the first place.

Summary
Congratulations!

You have completed the academic portion of SSI Enriched Air Nitrox Diver 40.

To dive EAN40, you will have to pass a final performance review.

Diving nitrox opens the door to opportunities that are not available to recreational divers using air. It can require a somewhat greater expenditure of resources than diving air does, but if you poll those divers who have discovered the world of EANx diving, the general consensus would be, "It's worth it."

Section 4 Review Questions

1. The way in which planning nitrox dives differs most from planning air dives is that, when diving EANx, you must also manage your exposure to _____.

2. Most nitrox-programmable dive computers not only track a diver's exposure to _____, they also track the diver's exposure to _____.

3. Using the SSI Equivalent Air Depth table, determine the equivalent air depth (EAD) for the following depths using EAN32:
Dive 1: 100 ft/30 m. EAD is _____.
Dive 2: 50 ft/15 m. EAD is _____.

4. The smallest PO_2 value on the SSI CNS "Clock" Exposure Time Table is _____. A conservative approach to tracking oxygen exposure is to treat dives with a PO_2 of _____ and less as if they equal to _____ .

5. Using the SSI Equivalent Air Depth table, determine the equivalent air depth (EAD) for the following depths using EAN36:
Dive 1: 90 ft/27 m. EAD is _____.
Dive 2: 80 ft/24 m. EAD is _____.

6. The single most important aspect of limiting your exposure to oxygen is keeping within _____ PO_2 levels. This is why, throughout this manual, we've advised you to remain within a limiting PO_2 of _____ atmospheres or less.

7. Remember that, even though you may use an _____ computer or dive table when diving nitrox, you must still take steps to ensure your exposure to _____ does not exceed acceptable levels.

8. EAD is another way of saying, "If you breathe a particular _____ mixture at this depth, you will expose your body to the same overall level of _____ as you would experience when breathing _____ at this shallower depth."

9. If your goal is to _____ safety, you will want to plan your dives using either an _____ dive computer or the SSI _____ Dive Tables. However, as mentioned earlier in this section, doing so does not eliminate the need to keep your exposure to _____ within recommended limits.

10. On the other hand, if your goal is to _____ _____ _____ , your choice of planning tools will include _____ _____ _____ _____ or a combination of the SSI Tables.

11. Many nitrox divers like to take at least _____ _____ surface interval between nitrox dives and any other subsequent air dives.

Appendix

Introduction

The SSI Enriched Air Nitrox program trains divers to use EANx within normal recreational diving limits. As with all recreational diving programs, it is designed to keep the subject matter as simple and uncomplicated as possible.

At some point, however, you may want to expand your knowledge and experience beyond the recreational level. Doing so may involve taking part in one or more technical diver training programs. As part of these programs, you will be expected to develop a greater understanding of the physics and physiology of diving. This may require that you be able to solve a variety of formulas to determine factors such as partial pressure of oxygen (PO_2), equivalent air depth (EAD) and maximum operating depth (MOD). You may also want this ability simply to satisfy a curiosity regarding where the numbers you find throughout this manual come from.

Here in the Appendix, we present the formulas and their conversions used to develop the tables and charts appearing throughout the book, along with an explanation as to what each of the variables represent. You may find yourself using these, or similar formulas, in later diver training programs.

Note

All of the formulas appearing here use depth values for salt water. To solve these formulas using depth values for fresh water, substitute 34 feet for 33 feet when working with imperial measurements. Substitute 10.3 metres for 10.0 metres if working their metric equivalents. For simplicity, these formulas assume that 33 feet or 10 metres of salt water exert a pressure precisely equal to either one atmosphere or one bar.

Enriched Air Nitrox
Partial Pressure of Oxygen (PO$_2$)

Partial Pressure = Depth in   X   Fraction of
of Oxygen (PO$_2$)   Atmospheres   Oxygen (FO$_2$)

FEET

$$PO_2 = \left[\left(\frac{Depth}{33\,ft}\right) + 1\right] \times FO_2$$

METRES

$$PO_2 = \left[\left(\frac{Depth}{10\,m}\right) + 1\right] \times FO_2$$

**The formulas for determining partial pressure of oxygen (PO$_2$).
Use the top formula for feet; the bottom formula for metres.**

The formulas for determining the partial pressure of oxygen (PO$_2$) appear in the diagram above.

In these formulas, d is a variable representing a depth in either feet or metres of salt water. The portion of the equation in parentheses, by itself, can be used to determine absolute pressure at depth in either atmospheres or bar.

Enriched Air Nitrox
Equivalent Air Depth (EAD)

FEET

$$EAD = \left(\frac{(1 - FO_2) \times (D + 33)}{0.79} \right) - 33$$

METRES

$$EAD = \left(\frac{(1 - FO_2) \times (D + 10)}{0.79} \right) - 10$$

Equivalent air depth (EAD) formulas. Use the top formula for imperial values; the bottom for metric values.

The formula above can be used to find the equivalent air depth when actual depth is known.

This formula is of greatest value if the maximum possible depth of a dive is known, and one wanted to use this knowledge to calculate the most precise equivalent air depth possible. The variable D represents actual depth in feet or metres.

Enriched Air Nitrox
Actual Depth (from EAD)

$$\text{FEET} \qquad D = \frac{0.79\,(EAD + 33)}{(1 - FO_2)} - 33$$

$$\text{METRES} \qquad D = \frac{0.79\,(EAD + 10)}{(1 - FO_2)} - 10$$

Actual depth formulas. Use the top formula for imperial values;
the bottom for metric values.

The diagram above depicts the formulas used to determine the actual nitrox depth if the equivalent air depth is known.

These are the formulas used to generate the SSI Equivalent Depth table.

Enriched Air Nitrox
Maximum Operating Depth (MOD)

$$\text{FEET} \qquad MOD = \left(\frac{33 \times (PO_2)}{(FO_2)} \right) - 33$$

$$\text{METRES} \qquad MOD = \left(\frac{10 \times (PO_2)}{(FO_2)} \right) - 10$$

Maximum operating depth (MOD) formulas. Use the top formula
for imperial values; the bottom for metric values.

The diagram above depicts the formulas used to determine the maximum operating depth (MOD) when the limiting PO_2 and oxygen concentration of the gas mixture being breathed are known.

It is generally easier to obtain MOD information by consulting a table.

COMBINED AIR/EANx DIVE TABLES
DOPPLER NO-DECOMPRESSION LIMITS BASED ON U.S. NAVY DIVE TABLES

SSI
SCUBA SCHOOLS INTERNATIONAL

TABLE 1 — No-Decompression Limits and Repetitive Group Designation Table For No-Decompression Dives

HOW TO USE TABLE 1: *Find the planned depth of your dive in feet at the far left of Table 1. Read to the right until you find the time (minutes) you plan to spend at that depth. Read down to find the Group Designation letter.*

DEPTH IN FEET — AIR PO₂	EAN32 PO₂	EAN36 PO₂	DOPPLER LIMITS (minutes)											
10 / 0.27	16 / 0.48	20 / 0.58		60	120	210	300							
15 / 0.31	22 / 0.54	26 / 0.65		35	70	110	160	225	350					
20 / 0.34	28 / 0.60	32 / 0.71		25	50	75	100	135	180	240	325			
25 / 0.37	34 / 0.65	38 / 0.78	245	20	35	55	75	100	125	160	195	245		
30 / 0.40	40 / 0.76	44 / 0.85	205	15	30	45	60	75	95	120	145	170	205	
35 / 0.43	46 / 0.77	50 / 0.92	160	5	15	25	40	50	60	80	100	120	140	160
40 / 0.47	51 / 0.82	57 / 0.98	130	5	15	25	30	40	50	70	80	100	110	130
50 / 0.53	63 / 0.94	69 / 1.12	70		10	15	25	30	40	50	60	70		
60 / 0.59	75 / 1.05	81 / 1.25	50		10	15	20	25	30	40	50			
70 / 0.66	86 / 1.16	94 / 1.39	40			5	10	15	20	30	35	40		
80 / 0.72	98 / 1.27	106 / 1.52	30			5	10	15	20	25	30			
90 / 0.78	109 / 1.39		25			5	10	12	15	20	25			
100 / 0.85	121 / 1.50		20			5	7	10	15	20				
110 / 0.91	130 / 1.58		15			5	10	13	15					
120 / 0.97			10			5	10							
130 / 1.04			5			5								

GROUP DESIGNATION: A B C D E F G H I J K

HOW TO USE TABLE 2:

Enter with the Group Designation letter from Table 1. Follow the arrow down to the corresponding letter on Table 2. To the left of these letters are windows of time. Read to the left until you find the times between which your surface interval falls. Then read down until you find your New Group Designation letter. Dives following surface intervals of more than 12 hours are not repetitive dives.

TABLE 2 — Residual Nitrogen Timetable For Repetitive Dives

REPETITIVE GROUP AT THE BEGINNING OF THE SURFACE INTERVAL

A	B	C	D	E	F	G	H	I	J	K
0:10 / 12:00*										
3:21 / 12:00*	0:10 / 3:20									
4:50 / 12:00*	1:40 / 4:49	0:10 / 1:39								
5:49 / 12:00*	2:39 / 5:48	1:10 / 2:38	0:10 / 1:09							
6:35 / 12:00*	3:25 / 6:34	1:58 / 3:24	0:55 / 1:57	0:10 / 0:54						
7:06 / 12:00*	3:58 / 7:05	2:29 / 3:57	1:30 / 2:28	0:46 / 1:29	0:10 / 0:45					
7:36 / 12:00*	4:26 / 7:35	2:59 / 4:25	2:00 / 2:58	1:16 / 1:59	0:41 / 1:15	0:10 / 0:40				
8:00 / 12:00*	4:50 / 7:59	3:21 / 4:49	2:24 / 3:20	1:42 / 2:23	1:07 / 1:41	0:37 / 1:06	0:10 / 0:36			
8:22 / 12:00*	5:13 / 8:21	3:44 / 5:12	2:45 / 3:43	2:03 / 2:44	1:30 / 2:02	1:00 / 1:29	0:34 / 0:59	0:10 / 0:33		
8:51 / 12:00*	5:41 / 8:50	4:03 / 5:40	3:05 / 4:02	2:21 / 3:04	1:48 / 2:20	1:20 / 1:47	0:55 / 1:19	0:32 / 0:54	0:10 / 0:31	
8:59 / 12:00*	5:49 / 8:58	4:20 / 5:48	3:22 / 4:19	2:39 / 3:21	2:04 / 2:38	1:36 / 2:03	1:12 / 1:35	0:50 / 1:11	0:29 / 0:49	0:10 / 0:28

NEW GROUP DESIGNATION ►	A	B	C	D	E	F	G	H	I	J	K

REPETITIVE DIVE DEPTH ▼ ▼RESIDUAL NITROGEN TIMES DISPLAYED ON REVERSE▼

© 1996 CONCEPT SYSTEMS. INC.

Reorder N° 2206EAN

SSI Combined Air/EANx Dive Tables in feet (front).

COMBINED AIR/EANx DIVE TABLES
DOPPLER NO-DECOMPRESSION LIMITS BASED ON U.S. NAVY DIVE TABLES

TABLE 3 — Residual Nitrogen Times (Minutes)
— CONTINUED FROM REVERSE SIDE —

NEW GROUP DESIGNATION ▶

■ =ADJUSTED NO-DECOMPRESSION TIME LIMITS   N/L=NO LIMIT

REPETITIVE DIVE DEPTH IN FEET — AIR PO₂	EAN32 PO₂	EAN36 PO₂	A	B	C	D	E	F	G	H	I	J	K
10 / 0.27	16 / 0.48	20 / 0.58	39	88	159	279							
			N/L	N/L	N/L	N/L							
20 / 0.34	28 / 0.60	32 / 0.71	18	39	62	88	120	159	208	279	399		
			N/L	N/L	N/L	N/L	N/L	N/L	N/L	N/L	N/L		
30 / 0.40	40 / 0.71	44 / 0.85	12	25	39	54	70	88	109	132	159	190	
			193	180	166	151	135	117	96	73	46	15	
40 / 0.47	51 / 0.82	57 / 0.98	7	17	25	37	49	61	73	87	101	116	
			123	113	105	93	81	69	57	43	29	14	
50 / 0.53	63 / 0.94	69 / 1.12	6	13	21	29	38	47	56	66			
			64	57	49	41	32	23	14	4			
60 / 0.59	75 / 1.05	81 / 1.25	5	11	17	24	30	36	44				
			45	39	33	26	20	14	6				
70 / 0.66	86 / 1.16	94 / 1.39	4	9	15	20	26	31	37				
			36	31	25	20	14	9	3				
80 / 0.72	98 / 1.27	106 / 1.52	4	8	13	18	23	28					
			26	22	17	12	7	2					
90 / 0.78	109 / 1.39		3	7	11	16	20	24					
			22	18	14	9	5	1					
100 / 0.85	121 / 1.50		3	7	10	14	18						
			17	13	10	6	2						
110 / 0.91	130 / 1.58		3	6	10	13							
			12	9	5	2							
120 / 0.97			3	6	9								
			7	4	1								
130 / 1.04			3										
			2										

HOW TO USE TABLE 3:
Enter with the New Group Designation letter from Table 2. Next, find the planned depth of your repetitive dive in feet at the far left of Table 3. The box that intersects the Repetitive Dive Depth and the New Group Designation will have two numbers. The top number indicates the Residual Nitrogen Time. The bottom number indicates the maximum Adjusted No-Decompression Time Limit for the next dive.

1 RG   RG   SI   RG ➡ (for next dive this day)
D ____   safety stop ☐ ____ ft. (m.)
RT ____
BT ____
TT ____

Computer Dive (fill out color items)
End PSI(Bar): ____ Used: ____
SAC = ____ psi/min. (bar/min.)   Ascent OK: ☐

2 RG   RG   SI   RG ➡ (for next dive this day)
D ____   safety stop ☐ ____ ft. (m.)
RT ____
BT ____
TT ____

Computer Dive (fill out color items)
End PSI(Bar): ____ Used: ____
SAC = ____ psi/min. (bar/min.)   Ascent OK: ☐

WARNING: *The U.S. Navy Dive Tables were designed to Navy specifications for use by Navy Divers. When used by recreational divers, the tables should be used conservatively. Even when used correctly with proper safety procedures, **decompression sickness may still occur.***

SAFETY STOP PROCEDURE: *It is recommended that you make a 3- to 5-minute safety stop at 15 feet on all dives over 30 feet.*

OMITTED DECOMPRESSION PROCEDURE: *Should you exceed the Doppler No-Decompression Time Limits by less than 5 minutes on any dive, it is recommended that you ascend normally to 15 feet and stop for at least 10 minutes or longer if your air supply allows. Should you exceed the Doppler No-Decompression Time Limits by more than 5 minutes but less than 10 minutes on any dive, it is recommended that you stop at 15 feet for at least 20 minutes or longer if your air supply allows.*
Refrain from any further scuba diving activities for at least 24 hours.

Reorder Nº 2206EAN

SSI Combined Air/EANx Dive Tables in feet (back).

COMBINED AIR/EANX DIVE TABLES *SSI*
SCUBA SCHOOLS INTERNATIONAL
DOPPLER NO-DECOMPRESSION LIMITS BASED ON U.S. NAVY DIVE TABLES

TABLE 1 — No-Decompression Limits and Repetitive Group Designation Table For No-Decompression Dives

HOW TO USE TABLE 1: *Find the planned depth of your dive in metres at the far left of Table 1. Read to the right until you find the time (minutes) you plan to spend at that depth. Read down to find the Group Designation letter.*

AIR PO₂	EAN32 PO₂	EAN36 PO₂	Doppler limits (minutes)	A	B	C	D	E	F	G	H	I	J	K
3 / 0.27	5 / 0.48	6 / 0.58		60	120	210	300							
4.5 / 0.30	6 / 0.51	8 / 0.65		35	70	110	160	225	350					
6 / 0.34	8 / 0.58	9 / 0.68		25	50	75	100	135	180	240	325			
7.5 / 0.37	10 / 0.64	11 / 0.76	245	20	35	55	75	100	125	160	195	245		
9 / 0.40	12 / 0.70	13 / 0.83	205	15	30	45	60	75	95	120	145	170	205	
10 / 0.42	13 / 0.74	15 / 0.90	160	5	15	25	40	50	60	80	100	120	140	160
12 / 0.46	16 / 0.83	17 / 0.97	130	5	15	25	30	40	50	70	80	100	110	130
15 / 0.53	19 / 0.93	21 / 1.12	70	10	15	25	30	40	50	60	70			
18 / 0.59	23 / 1.06	25 / 1.26	50	10	15	20	25	30	40	50				
21 / 0.65	26 / 1.15	28 / 1.37	40	5	10	15	20	30	35	40				
24 / 0.71	30 / 1.28	32 / 1.51	30	5	10	15	20	25	30					
27 / 0.78	33 / 1.38		25	5	10	12	15	20	25					
30 / 0.84	37 / 1.50		20	5	7	10	15	20						
34 / 0.92	40 / 1.60		15	5	10	13	15							
37 / 0.99			10	5	10									
40 / 1.05			5	5										

GROUP DESIGNATION: A B C D E F G H I J K

TABLE 2 — Residual Nitrogen Timetable For Repetitive Dives

HOW TO USE TABLE 2: *Enter with the Group Designation letter from Table 1. Follow the arrow down to the corresponding letter on Table 2. To the left of these letters are windows of time. Read to the left until you find the times between which your surface interval falls. Then read down until you find your New Group Designation letter. Dives following surface intervals of more than 12 hours are not repetitive dives.*

REPETITIVE GROUP AT THE BEGINNING OF THE SURFACE INTERVAL

	A	B	C	D	E	F	G	H	I	J	K
A	0:10 / 12:00*										
B	3:21 / 12:00*	0:10 / 3:20									
C	4:50 / 12:00*	1:40 / 4:49	0:10 / 1:39								
D	5:49 / 12:00*	2:39 / 5:48	1:10 / 2:38	0:10 / 1:09							
E	6:35 / 12:00*	3:25 / 6:34	1:58 / 3:24	0:55 / 1:57	0:10 / 0:54						
F	7:06 / 12:00*	3:58 / 7:05	2:29 / 3:57	1:30 / 2:28	0:46 / 1:29	0:10 / 0:45					
G	7:36 / 12:00*	4:26 / 7:35	2:59 / 4:25	2:00 / 2:58	1:16 / 1:59	0:41 / 1:15	0:10 / 0:40				
H	8:00 / 12:00*	4:50 / 7:59	3:21 / 4:49	2:24 / 3:20	1:42 / 2:23	1:07 / 1:41	0:37 / 1:06	0:10 / 0:36			
I	8:22 / 12:00*	5:13 / 8:21	3:44 / 5:12	2:45 / 3:43	2:03 / 2:44	1:30 / 2:02	1:00 / 1:29	0:34 / 0:59	0:10 / 0:33		
J	8:51 / 12:00*	5:41 / 8:50	4:03 / 5:40	3:05 / 4:02	2:21 / 3:04	1:48 / 2:20	1:20 / 1:47	0:55 / 1:19	0:32 / 0:54	0:10 / 0:31	
K	8:59 / 12:00*	5:49 / 8:58	4:20 / 5:48	3:22 / 4:19	2:39 / 3:21	2:04 / 2:38	1:36 / 2:03	1:12 / 1:35	0:50 / 1:11	0:29 / 0:49	0:10 / 0:28

NEW GROUP DESIGNATION ▶ A B C D E F G H I J K

REPETITIVE DIVE DEPTH ▼ ▼ RESIDUAL NITROGEN TIMES DISPLAYED ON REVERSE ▼

ADRO:SSI:EDU:SPEC:EANx:SLATES•1065EANB_0306_SSI_EANxDvTbls•Reorder N° 2206M-EAN

SSI Combined Air/EANx Dive Tables in metres (front).

COMBINED AIR/EANX DIVE TABLES

DOPPLER NO-DECOMPRESSION LIMITS BASED ON U.S. NAVY DIVE TABLES

TABLE 3 — Residual Nitrogen Times (Minutes)

— CONTINUED FROM REVERSE SIDE —

NEW GROUP DESIGNATION ▶

■ =ADJUSTED NO-DECOMPRESSION TIME LIMITS   N/L=NO LIMIT

REPETITIVE DIVE DEPTH IN METRES — AIR PO₂	EAN32 PO₂	EAN36 PO₂	A	B	C	D	E	F	G	H	I	J	K
3 / 0.27	5 / 0.48	6 / 0.58	39	88	159	279							
			N/L	N/L	N/L	N/L							
6 / 0.34	8 / 0.58	9 / 0.68	18	39	62	88	120	159	208	279	399		
			N/L	N/L	N/L	N/L	N/L	N/L	N/L	N/L	N/L		
9 / 0.40	12 / 0.70	13 / 0.83	12	25	39	54	70	88	109	132	159	190	
			193	180	166	151	135	117	96	73	46	15	
12 / 0.46	16 / 0.83	17 / 0.97	7	17	25	37	49	61	73	87	101	116	
			123	113	105	93	81	69	57	43	29	14	
15 / 0.53	19 / 0.93	21 / 1.12	6	13	21	29	38	47	56	66			
			64	57	49	41	32	23	14	4			
18 / 0.59	23 / 1.06	25 / 1.26	5	11	17	24	30	36	44				
			45	39	33	26	20	14	6				
21 / 0.65	26 / 1.15	28 / 1.37	4	9	15	20	26	31	37				
			36	31	25	20	14	9	3				
24 / 0.71	30 / 1.28	32 / 1.51	4	8	13	18	23	28					
			26	22	17	12	7	2					
27 / 0.78	33 / 1.38		3	7	11	16	20	24					
			22	18	14	9	5	1					
30 / 0.84	37 / 1.50		3	7	10	14	18						
			17	13	10	6	2						
34 / 0.92	40 / 1.60		3	6	10	13							
			12	9	5	2							
37 / 0.99			3	6	9								
			7	4	1								
40 / 1.05			3										
			2										

HOW TO USE TABLE 3:

Enter with the New Group Designation letter from Table 2. Next, find the planned depth of your repetitive dive in metres at the far left of Table 3. The box that intersects the Repetitive Dive Depth and the New Group Designation will have two numbers. The top number indicates the Residual Nitrogen Time. The bottom number indicates the maximum Adjusted No-Decompression Time Limit for the next dive.

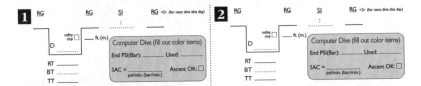

WARNING: The U.S. Navy Dive Tables were designed to Navy specifications for use by Navy Divers. When used by recreational divers, the tables should be used conservatively. Even when used correctly with proper safety procedures, **decompression sickness may still occur.**

SAFETY STOP PROCEDURE: It is recommended that you make a 3- to 5-minute safety stop at 5 metres on all dives over 9 metres.

OMITTED DECOMPRESSION PROCEDURE: Should you exceed the Doppler No-Decompression Time Limits by less than 5 minutes on any dive, it is recommended that you ascend normally to 5 metres and stop for at least 10 minutes or longer if your air supply allows. Should you exceed the Doppler No-Decompression Time Limits by more than 5 minutes but less than 10 minutes on any dive, it is recommended that you stop at 5 metres for at least 20 minutes or longer if your air supply allows.

Refrain from any further scuba diving activities for at least 24 hours.

© 1996 CONCEPT SYSTEMS, INC., Rev. 3/06   ADRO:SSI:EDU:SPEC:EANx:SLATES•1065EANB_0306_SSI_EANxDvTbls•Reorder N° 2206M-EAN

SSI Combined Air/EANx Dive Tables in metres (back).

SSI Equivalent Air Depth Table Use

SSI Equivalent Depth table is shown on page A-12 (feet) and page A-13 (metres). This table provides EAD information for depths from 35-130 feet/10-42 metres, and for FO$_2$ from 22-36 percent.

Using the Equivalent Depth table will be familiar to anyone who has ever used a conversion table for altitude diving. You begin by finding the column that corresponds to the FO$_2$ of the gas you are breathing. Moving downward, you find the depth value that is equal to, or just slightly deeper than the maximum depth of the dive. Moving to the left, you find the equivalent depth value to use in conjunction with your air-based dive table.

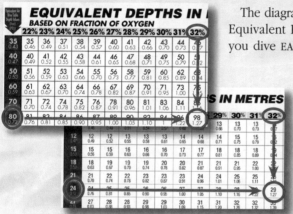

Shown in feet and metres.

The diagrams to the left show how the Equivalent Depth table works. Let's say you dive EAN32, and go to a depth that approaches, but does not exceed 98 feet/29 metres. Following the table down and across, you discover that you can treat this as an air dive to 80 feet/24 metres, using your air-based dive table.

Now let's say that on a subsequent dive you use EAN26 and reach a depth that approaches, but does not exceed 66 feet/20 metres. As this example illustrates, you can treat this as an air dive to 60 feet/18 metres, using your air-based dive table.

During your nitrox diver program, your SSI Instructor will help you work several other example problems using the SSI Equivalent Depth Table, and whatever air-based dive tables you normally use when diving air.

Shown in feet and metres.

EQUIVALENT DEPTHS IN FEET
BASED ON FRACTION OF OXYGEN

SSI SCUBA SCHOOLS INTERNATIONAL

Equivalent Air Table Depth Values [Feet] (PO2)

(PO2)	22%	23%	24%	25%	26%	27%	28%	29%	30%	31%	32%	33%	34%	35%	36%	37%	38%	39%	40%
35 0.43	35 / 0.46	36 / 0.49	37 / 0.51	38 / 0.54	39 / 0.57	40 / 0.60	41 / 0.63	42 / 0.66	43 / 0.70	44 / 0.73	46 / 0.77	47 / 0.80	48 / 0.84	49 / 0.88	51 / 0.92	52 / 0.96	54 / 1.00	55 / 1.04	57 / 1.09
40 0.47	40 / 0.49	41 / 0.52	42 / 0.55	43 / 0.58	44 / 0.61	46 / 0.65	47 / 0.68	48 / 0.71	49 / 0.75	50 / 0.79	51 / 0.82	53 / 0.86	54 / 0.90	55 / 0.94	57 / 0.98	59 / 1.03	60 / 1.07	62 / 1.12	63 / 1.17
50 0.53	51 / 0.56	52 / 0.59	53 / 0.63	54 / 0.66	55 / 0.70	56 / 0.73	58 / 0.77	59 / 0.81	60 / 0.85	62 / 0.89	63 / 0.94	64 / 0.98	66 / 1.02	67 / 1.07	69 / 1.12	71 / 1.17	73 / 1.22	74 / 1.27	76 / 1.32
60 0.59	61 / 0.63	62 / 0.67	63 / 0.70	64 / 0.74	66 / 0.78	67 / 0.82	69 / 0.87	70 / 0.91	71 / 0.95	73 / 1.00	75 / 1.05	76 / 1.10	78 / 1.15	80 / 1.20	82 / 1.25	84 / 1.31	86 / 1.36	87 / 1.42	89 / 1.48
70 0.66	71 / 0.70	72 / 0.74	74 / 0.78	75 / 0.82	76 / 0.87	78 / 0.91	80 / 0.96	81 / 1.01	83 / 1.06	84 / 1.11	86 / 1.16	88 / 1.21	90 / 1.27	92 / 1.33	94 / 1.39	96 / 1.45	98 / 1.51	100 / 1.58	
80 0.72	81 / 0.76	82 / 0.81	84 / 0.85	86 / 0.90	87 / 0.95	89 / 1.00	90 / 1.05	92 / 1.10	94 / 1.16	96 / 1.22	98 / 1.27	100 / 1.33	102 / 1.39	104 / 1.46	106 / 1.52				
90 0.78	91 / 0.83	93 / 0.88	94 / 0.93	96 / 0.98	98 / 1.03	100 / 1.09	101 / 1.15	103 / 1.20	105 / 1.26	107 / 1.32	109 / 1.39	112 / 1.45	114 / 1.52	116 / 1.59					
100 0.85	101 / 0.90	103 / 0.95	105 / 1.01	107 / 1.06	108 / 1.12	110 / 1.18	112 / 1.24	114 / 1.30	117 / 1.36	119 / 1.43	121 / 1.50	123 / 1.57							
110 0.91	111 / 0.97	113 / 1.02	115 / 1.08	117 / 1.14	119 / 1.20	121 / 1.27	123 / 1.33	126 / 1.40	128 / 1.47	130 / 1.54	130 / 1.58								
120 0.97	121 / 1.03	123 / 1.09	126 / 1.16	128 / 1.22	130 / 1.29	132 / 1.35	134 / 1.42	137 / 1.50	139 / 1.57										
130 1.04	132 / 1.10	134 / 1.17	136 / 1.23	138 / 1.30	141 / 1.37	143 / 1.44	145 / 1.52	148 / 1.59											

Legend:
- ▢ = PO2 in excess of 1.4 ATA/bar
- ▣ = PO2 in excess of 1.5 ATA/bar

Example:
32% — Fraction of Oxygen (FO2)
98 — Actual Depth
127 — Partial Pressure of Oxygen (PO2)

⚠ WARNING

■ Enriched Air Nitrox (EANx) diving entails additional risks not present when diving air, including the risk of Central Nervous System (CNS) oxygen toxicity, which can lead to loss of consciousness, under water, resulting in *serious personal injury or death.* Obtain special training and certification from a qualified instructor before diving Nitrox.

■ Use dive tables and other planning tools conservatively and correctly. Be aware, however, that even if you do so, decompression sickness or CNS oxygen toxicity may still occur.

1865C_0909_SSI_EANAirDpthSite

Consult SSI Nitrox Diver Manual for detailed instructions on use of this table. • Reorder Nº 2506EAN

© 1996 CONCEPT SYSTEMS, INC.

SSI Equivalent Depth table (in feet).

EQUIVALENT DEPTHS IN METRES
BASED ON FRACTION OF OXYGEN

SSI — SCUBA SCHOOLS INTERNATIONAL

Each cell shows Equivalent Depth (metres) over Partial Pressure of Oxygen (PO_2).

Equivalent Air Dive Table Depth Values (Feet) (PO_2)	22%	23%	24%	25%	26%	27%	28%	29%	30%	31%	32%	33%	34%	35%	36%	37%	38%	39%	40%
10 (0.42)	10 / 0.44	11 / 0.48	11 / 0.50	11 / 0.53	11 / 0.55	12 / 0.59	12 / 0.62	12 / 0.64	13 / 0.69	13 / 0.71	13 / 0.74	14 / 0.79	14 / 0.82	14 / 0.84	15 / 0.90	16 / 0.96	16 / 0.99	17 / 1.05	17 / 1.08
12 (0.46)	12 / 0.48	13 / 0.53	13 / 0.55	13 / 0.58	13 / 0.60	14 / 0.65	14 / 0.67	14 / 0.70	15 / 0.75	15 / 0.78	16 / 0.83	16 / 0.86	16 / 0.88	17 / 0.95	17 / 0.97	18 / 1.04	18 / 1.06	19 / 1.13	19 / 1.16
15 (0.53)	15 / 0.55	16 / 0.60	16 / 0.62	16 / 0.65	17 / 0.70	17 / 0.73	17 / 0.76	18 / 0.81	18 / 0.84	19 / 0.90	19 / 0.93	19 / 0.96	20 / 1.02	20 / 1.05	21 / 1.12	22 / 1.18	22 / 1.22	23 / 1.29	23 / 1.32
18 (0.59)	18 / 0.62	19 / 0.67	19 / 0.70	19 / 0.73	20 / 0.78	20 / 0.81	21 / 0.87	21 / 0.90	22 / 0.96	22 / 0.99	23 / 1.06	23 / 1.09	24 / 1.16	24 / 1.19	25 / 1.26	26 / 1.33	26 / 1.37	26 / 1.40	27 / 1.48
21 (0.65)	21 / 0.68	22 / 0.74	22 / 0.77	23 / 0.83	23 / 0.86	24 / 0.92	24 / 0.95	24 / 0.99	25 / 1.05	25 / 1.09	26 / 1.15	27 / 1.22	27 / 1.26	28 / 1.33	28 / 1.37	29 / 1.44	30 / 1.52	30 / 1.56	
24 (0.71)	24 / 0.75	25 / 0.81	25 / 0.84	26 / 0.90	26 / 0.94	27 / 1.00	27 / 1.04	28 / 1.10	28 / 1.14	29 / 1.21	30 / 1.28	30 / 1.32	31 / 1.39	31 / 1.44	32 / 1.51	33 / 1.59			
27 (0.78)	27 / 0.81	28 / 0.87	28 / 0.91	29 / 0.98	30 / 1.04	30 / 1.08	31 / 1.15	31 / 1.19	32 / 1.26	32 / 1.30	33 / 1.38	34 / 1.45	34 / 1.50	35 / 1.58					
30 (0.84)	31 / 0.90	31 / 0.94	32 / 1.01	32 / 1.05	33 / 1.12	33 / 1.16	34 / 1.23	35 / 1.31	35 / 1.35	36 / 1.43	37 / 1.50	37 / 1.55							
34 (0.92)	34 / 0.97	34 / 1.01	35 / 1.08	35 / 1.13	36 / 1.20	37 / 1.27	37 / 1.32	38 / 1.39	39 / 1.47	39 / 1.52	40 / 1.60								
37 (0.99)	37 / 1.03	37 / 1.08	38 / 1.15	38 / 1.20	39 / 1.27	40 / 1.35	40 / 1.40	41 / 1.48											
40 (1.05)	40 / 1.10	40 / 1.15	41 / 1.22	42 / 1.30	42 / 1.35	43 / 1.43	44 / 1.51	45 / 1.60											

Legend:
- ■ = PO_2 in excess of 1.4 ATA/bar
- ■ = PO_2 in excess of 1.5 ATA/bar

Example key: 32% = Fraction of Oxygen (FO_2); 30 = Actual Depth; 1.28 = Partial Pressure of Oxygen (PO_2).

⚠ **WARNING**
- Enriched Air Nitrox (EANx) diving entails additional risks not present when diving air, including the risk of Central Nervous System (CNS) oxygen toxicity, which can lead to loss of consciousness under water, resulting in serious personal injury or death. Obtain special training and certification from a qualified instructor before diving Nitrox.
- Use dive tables and other planning tools conservatively and correctly. Be aware, however, that even if you do so, decompression sickness or CNS oxygen toxicity may still occur.

© 1996 CONCEPT SYSTEMS, INC. • Reorder Nº 2506EAN

Consult SSI Nitrox Diver Manual for detailed instructions on use of this table.

1865C_0909_SSI_EANxrDpthSite

SSI Equivalent Depth table (in metres).

Although you should take both the Equivalent Depth table and your air-based dive table with you on every dive, it may be helpful to do some additional preparation work.

The graphic to the right shows the type of data you may want to enter on your slate prior to an EANx dive. This example assumes you will be diving EAN30. The first column contains depth values (in feet and metres) from the 30 percent column on the Equivalent

EAN30	AIR	NDL
60′	50′	70
71′	60′	50
83′	70′	40
94′	80′	30
105′	90′	25

EAN30	AIR	NDL
18m	15m	70
21m	18m	50
25m	21m	40
28m	24m	30
32m	27m	25

Pre-planning no-decompression limits based on FO₂.

Depth table. Not every depth from this column appears, just enough to cover the anticipated range of the dive.

The second column shows the EADs for the depths appearing in the first column. The third column shows the no-decompression limits for the air depths in the second column — in this case, the Doppler limits from the SSI Dive Tables. This type of preparation may not only save you time at the end of the dive, it may also help you better plan your dive.

The Equivalent Depth table enables you to use the same dive tables you are already familiar with for air and EANx at any common FO₂. When using this table, however, there are a few things you should be aware of.

◆ For simplicity and ease of use, the depth values appearing on the table have been rounded to the next shallower number that is a whole integer (i.e., 29 metres instead of 29.96 metres).

◆ Most of the depth values appearing on the Equivalent Depth table reflect a PO₂ of less than 1.4 atmospheres. Depth values that exceed this recommended limiting PO₂ appear in shaded boxes. These appear solely for contingency planning. You should not intentionally exceed a PO₂ of 1.4 atmospheres. No values appear for depths whose PO₂ exceeds the maximum limiting PO₂ of 1.6 atmospheres.

◆ The deepest depth appearing in an unshaded box in any column is not necessarily the theoretical maximum operating depth (MOD). For example, when diving EAN32, you actually hit the recommended limiting PO₂ of 1.4 atmospheres at 111 feet

Shown in feet and metres.

(34 metres) — not 109 feet (33 metres) as appears on the table. Nevertheless, these depth values are sufficiently close that they can be used as the effective MOD for any dive, without having to consult additional tables or solve mathematical formulas.

There is no substantial degree of conservatism built into the Equivalent Depth table itself. You will need to employ the same safety factors you build into whatever air-based dive table you normally use. For example, if you use the SSI air-based Dive Tables, you want to take advantage of the fact these tables use no-decompression limits based on Doppler bubble studies, rather than the more liberal US Navy dive table limits.

Using the SSI Combined Air/EANx Dive Tables

Much of the time, nitrox divers breathe either EAN32, EAN36 or air. Even when divers re-fill a cylinder that previously contained EAN32 with air, for decompression limit planning purposes it is common to treat the resulting dilute mixture as though it was air. Thus, for many nitrox divers the most convenient dive planning tool may be the SSI Combined Air/EANx Dive Tables, shown on pages 4-14 through 4-17.

The Combined tables contain depth columns for both air, EAN32 and EAN36. The EAN32 and EAN36 columns contain much the same information as the 32 percent and 36 percent columns appearing on the SSI Equivalent Depth tables. Also included is PO$_2$ information, to help divers remain within safer limiting PO$_2$ and Maximum Operating Depths.

Using the Combined Air/EAN32 dive table is incredibly easy. Simply assume that any depth values appearing in the same row represent equivalent depths for dive planning purposes. For example, an EAN32 dive to 75 feet/23 metres can be considered the same as an air dive to 60 feet/18 metres.

Because the repetitive group designators (letter groups) on these tables represent the same overall level of nitrogen absorption, you can use the SSI Combined Air/EANx Dive Tables to switch back and forth

COMBINED A
DOPPLER NO-DECOMPRESS

TABLE 1 **No-Deco**
Designa

DEPTH (FEET)			DOPPLER LIMITS (minutes)
AIR PO$_2$	EAN32 PO$_2$	EAN36 PO$_2$	
10 0.27	15 0.38	20 0.58	
15 0.31	22 0.45	26 0.65	
20 0.34	28 0.53	32 0.71	
25 0.37	34 0.5	38 0.78	245
30 0.40	40 0.1	44 0.85	205
35 0.43	46 0.7	50 0.92	160
40 0.47	52	57 0.98	130
50 0.53	65	69 1.12	70
60 0.59	75 1.05	81 1.25	50
70 0.66	86 1.16	94 1.39	40
80 0.72	98 1.27	106 1.52	30
90	109		

OMBINED
LER NO-DECOMPR

No-De
Designa

METRES		Doppler limits (minutes)
EAN32 PO$_2$	EAN36 PO$_2$	
5 0.48	6 0.58	
6 0.51	8 0.65	
8 0.58	9 0.68	
10 0.64	11 0.76	245
12 0.70	13 0.83	205
13 0.74	15 0.90	160
16	17 0.97	130
23 1.06	21 1.12	70
	25 1.26	50
21 0.65	26 1.15	28 1.37	40
24 0.71	30 1.28	32 1.51	30
27	33		

Shown in feet and metres.

between dives made on nitrox, and dives made on air. During your nitrox diver program, your SSI Instructor will work through several example problems with you, showing how these tables work.

CNS "CLOCK" EXPOSURE TIME TABLE   SSI SCUBA SCHOOLS INTERNATIONAL

Partial Pressure of Oxygen (PO2)	Maximum Exposure Time in Minutes — Single Dive Limit	24-Hour Limit	— Actual Bottom Time in Minutes —											
			5	10	15	20	25	30	35	40	45	50	55	60
0.6	720	720	1%	1%	2%	3%	3%	4%	5%	6%	6%	7%	8%	8%
0.7	570	570	1%	2%	3%	4%	4%	5%	6%	7%	8%	9%	10%	11%
0.8	450	450	1%	2%	3%	4%	6%	7%	8%	9%	10%	11%	12%	13%
0.9	360	360	1%	3%	4%	6%	7%	8%	10%	11%	13%	14%	15%	17%
1.0	300	300	2%	3%	5%	7%	8%	10%	12%	13%	15%	17%	18%	20%
1.1	240	270	2%	4%	6%	8% / 7%	10% / 9%	13% / 11%	15% / 13%	17% / 15%	19% / 17%	21% / 19%	23% / 20%	25% / 22%
1.2	210	240	2%	5% / 4%	7% / 6%	10% / 8%	12% / 10%	14% / 13%	17% / 15%	19% / 17%	21% / 19%	24% / 21%	26% / 23%	29% / 25%
1.3	180	210	3% / 2%	6% / 5%	8% / 7%	11% / 10%	14% / 12%	17% / 14%	19% / 17%	22% / 19%	25% / 21%	28% / 24%	31% / 26%	33% / 29%
1.4	150	180	3%	7% / 6%	10% / 8%	13% / 11%	17% / 14%	20% / 17%	23% / 19%	27% / 22%	30% / 25%	33% / 28%	37% / 31%	40% / 33%
1.5	120	180	4% / 3%	8% / 6%	13% / 8%	17% / 11%	21% / 14%	25% / 17%	29% / 19%	33% / 22%	38% / 25%	42% / 28%	46% / 31%	50% / 33%
1.6	45	150	11% / 3%	22% / 7%	33% / 10%	44% / 13%	56% / 17%	67% / 20%	78% / 23%	89% / 27%	100% / 30%	111% / 33%	122% / 37%	133% / 40%

See reverse side for important warnings • Consult SSI Nitrox Diver Manual for detailed instructions on use of this table.
© 1996 CONCEPT SYSTEMS, INC. • Reorder Nº ????EAN (FEET) –or– 2506M-EAN (METRES)   1865C_0909_SSI_EANAirDpthSlte

CNS "Clock" Exposure Time Table.

The graphic above shows the SSI CNS "Clock" Exposure Time Table. Using this table is reasonably straightforward.

For each dive you make, determine the maximum PO_2 you encountered (as with using dive tables, you can simplify matters by assuming this was the PO_2 for the entire dive). Find this PO_2 value in the left-hand column and follow its row across until you find the column that corresponds to the actual bottom time of the dive (a shallow dive with a PO_2 of less than .5 atmospheres should be calculated as a .6 atmospheres dive for oxygen exposure tracking purposes). This will tell you what percentage of your CNS "clock" you used during the dive.

The total of all percentages for all dives within any 24-hour period should not exceed 100 percent.

EQUIVALENT DEPTHS
BASED ON FRACTION OF OXYGEN

Equivalent Air Dive Table Depth Values (Feet) (PO2)	22%	23%	24%	25%	26%	27%	28%	29%	30%	31
35 / 0.43	35 0.46	36 0.49	37 0.51	38 0.54	39 0.57	40 0.60	41 0.63	42 0.66	43 0.70	0.
40 / 0.47	40 0.49	41 0.52	42 0.55	43 0.58	44 0.61	46 0.65	47 0.68	48 0.71	49 0.75	5 0.
50 / 0.53	51 0.56	52 0.59	53 0.63	54 0.66	55 0.70	56 0.73	58 0.77	59 0.81	60 0.85	6 0.
60 / 0.59	61 0.63	62 0.67	63 0.70	64 0.74	66 0.78	67 0.82	69 0.87	70 0.91	71 0.95	7 1.
70 / 0.66	71 0.70	72 0.74	74 0.78	75 0.82	76 0.87	78 0.91	80 0.96	81 1.01	83 1.06	8 1.
80 / 0.72	81 0.76	82 0.81	84 0.85	86 0.90	87 0.95	89 1.00	90 1.05	92 1.10	94	9
90 / 0.78	91 0.83	93 0.88	94 0.93	96 0.98	98 1.03	100 1.09	101 1.15	103 1.20	106 1.26	1
100 / 0.85	101 0.90	103 0.95	105 1.01	107 1.06	108 1.12	110 1.18	112 1.24	114 1.30	117 1.36	1

PO_2 exposure within 1.4 ATM

CNS "CLOCK" EXPOS

Partial Pressure of Oxygen (PO2)	Maximum Exposure Time in Minutes		— A		
	Single Dive Limit	24-Hour Limit	5	10	15
0.6	720	720	1%	1%	2%
0.7	570	570	1%	2%	3%
0.8	450	450	1%	2%	3%
0.9	360	360	1%	3%	4%
1.0	300	300	2%	3%	5%
1.1	240	270	2%	4%	6%
1.2	210	240	2%	5% 4%	6%
1.3	180	210	3% 2%	6% 5%	8% 7%
1.4	150	180	3%	7% 6%	10% 8%
1.5	120	180	4% 3%	8% 6%	13% 8%
1.6	45	150	11% 3%	22%	33% 10%

Fifteen minutes at a PO_2 of 1.6 ATM
uses up 10 percent of your CNS "clock".

Here are two examples of how and why you might consult this table in real-world diving.

♦ On an EAN30 dive, you plan to go no deeper than the top of a particular wreck at 100 feet/30 metres, thus keeping your PO_2 exposure well within 1.4 atmospheres. However, during the dive you manage to drop an expensive light to the sand, which is at a depth of 130 feet/39 metres. Without thinking, you bounce down to retrieve the light and in so doing, increase your PO_2 exposure to 1.6 atmospheres.

Realizing you have exceeded your dive plan, you immediately begin a slow ascent and safety stop. Nevertheless, you understand that despite keeping your actual bottom time within the 15 minutes the tables allow for an equivalent air depth of 110 feet, your momentary exposure to a PO_2 of 1.6 atmospheres takes you outside the parameters of the simplified method of tracking O_2 exposure discussed earlier. What do you do now?

By consulting the table, you discover that a 15-minute exposure to a PO_2 of 1.6 atmospheres has caused you to use up 10 percent of your allowable CNS "clock." This still leaves you with 90 percent of your allowable exposure remaining. Assuming you remain within a limiting PO_2 of 1.4 atmospheres for all subsequent dives, this translates into more than 160 minutes of allowable CNS "clock" time remaining.

♦ After months of waiting, you finally find yourself aboard the live aboard dive vessel of your dreams — the one that allows you to make up to five (count 'em — five!) dives a day. Better still, they even have a nitrox blending station on board.

Upon reflection though, you realize this may present a problem. With your below-average gas consumption, many of these dives could easily exceed 40 minutes — giving you an accumulated actual bottom time for the day of in excess of 200 minutes. This is not exactly within the 180 minutes NOAA allows for a PO$_2$ of 1.4.

CNS "CLOCK" EXPOSURE TIM[E]

Partial Pressure of Oxygen (PO₂)	Maximum Exposure Time in Minutes		— Actual Bottom T					
	Single Dive Limit	24-Hour Limit	5	10	15	20	25	30
0.6	720	720	1%	1%	2%	3%	3%	4%
0.7	570	570	1%	2%	3%	4%	4%	5%
0.8	450	450	1%	2%	3%	4%	6%	7%
0.9	360	360	1%	3%	4%	6%	7%	8%
1.0	300	300	2%	3%	5%	7%	8%	10%
1.1	240	270	2%	4%	6%	8%	10%	13% 11%
1.2	210	240	2%	5%	7%	10%	12%	14% 13%
1.3	180	210	3%	6%	8%	11%	14%	17% 14%
1.4	150	180	3%	7%	10%	13%	17%	20% 17%

Thirty minutes at a PO$_2$ of 1.4 ATM uses up 17 percent of your CNS "clock".

To see where you stand, you start projecting how much of your CNS "clock" you are likely to use up on each dive. Your first dive of the day is likely to be a multi-level wall dive on EAN32. Assuming a PO$_2$ exposure of 1.4 atmospheres, thirty minutes of bottom time here will use up 17 percent of your "clock." Subsequent shallow reef dives, made on air, however, will each only use up about 7 percent of your "clock." What you see then, is that by staying within these parameters, you will only end up using less than 50 percent of your allowable "clock" time on any given day.

As you can tell from these examples, the odds of you ever exceeding your allowable CNS "clock" are very slim — especially if you remain within the recommended limiting PO$_2$ of 1.4 atmospheres. Still, should the need arise, the SSI CNS "Clock" Exposure Time Table provides the information needed to perform O$_2$ exposure calculations.

The Significance of Blending Methods

Although there are a wide variety of ways fill stations can create nitrox, the most significant question pertaining to the use of nitrox cylinders is, will the nitrox be pre-mixed before it enters the cylinder, or will this blending process occur inside the cylinder?

If the nitrox is blended prior to entering a scuba cylinder, and contains gas with an FO$_2$ of no more than 40 percent, no special scuba cylinder preparation or maintenance procedures may be required. Whether this is acceptable or not may also depend on local laws, regulations and standards of practice.

On the other hand, if the blending of nitrox is to occur inside the scuba cylinder itself, it is vital that the cylinder be O$_2$ clean and O$_2$ service rated. Why is this important? The first step for in-cylinder, partial-pressure blending of nitrox is to partially fill the cylinder with pure oxygen. If the cylinder or valve contains a build-up of hydrocarbons or other contaminants, or if non-oxygen-compatible lubricants or other components have been used in the valve, filling the cylinder with oxygen, under pressure, may substantially increase the risk of spontaneous combustion, resulting in a potentially lethal fire or explosion.

What do the Terms "O_2 Clean" and "O_2 Service Rated" Mean?

The term O_2 clean means that all components of the Air Delivery System or other equipment items have undergone a special cleaning process designed to remove any trace of hydrocarbon build-up, as well as any trace of grease or other non-oxygen-compatible contaminant. To meet the strictest definition of O_2 cleaning, the process must take place in a special "clean" room and, once treated, the affected item may never again be exposed to normal atmospheric air and the contaminants that air may contain.

In practice, however, it has proven sufficient for scuba equipment items to simply undergo the special cleaning process. They can then maintain their O_2 service rating, so long as they are used with cylinders that have been filled solely with gas mixtures containing oxygen-compatible air — a term we will discuss at greater length shortly.

The term O_2 service rated means that an item has not only been completely disassembled and subjected to the O_2 cleaning process, but also that it has been reassembled using only oxygen-compatible lubricants, o-rings and other components.

The Significance of Oxygen-Compatible Air

A key to maintaining the O_2 service rating of any equipment item is the use of oxygen-compatible air. Earlier in this section, we mentioned the fact that normal scuba air may still contain sufficient hydrocarbons and other contaminants to lead to dangerous build-ups on valve components and other surfaces. In contrast, oxygen-compatible air is air that has been subjected to a much more extensive filtering process, and is several times cleaner than that normally used to fill scuba cylinders.

Oxygen-Compatible Air

The use of oxygen-compatible air is essential to the partial-pressure blending process. Attempting to blend nitrox with air that is less than oxygen-compatible risks fire and explosion. Regardless of whether nitrox is created through in-cylinder, partial-pressure blending, pre-mixing or using semi-permeable membranes or similar devices, it is almost always created using oxygen-compatible air.

KNOWLEDGE · SKILLS · EQUIPMENT · EXPERIENCE
DIVER DIAMOND
SSI

As a nitrox diver, it is important you understand that, to maintain the O_2 service rating of your nitrox cylinders and any other items you may have had O_2 cleaned, you can expose them only to gas containing oxygen-compatible air. You may, for example, be able to have an O_2 clean and O_2 service rated cylinder re-filled with air—but only if that air meets the standards for oxygen compatibility. If you have such a cylinder filled with normal scuba air, it will lose its O_2 service rating. Worse, you may create a situation in which re-filling that cylinder with oxygen, during the partial-pressure blending process, creates the risk of fire or explosion.

In general, it's best to remember that most dive operators prefer you refill dedicated eanx cylinders only with nitrox.

It is essential that any cylinder used for in-cylinder, partial-pressure blending of nitrox be O_2 clean and O_2 service rated. Further, such cylinders may only be filled with pure oxygen or gases containing oxygen-compatible air. Additionally, nitrox blending should only be done by individuals possessing the special training and equipment required. Failure to follow these warnings may substantially increase the risk of fire or explosion which, in turn, can lead to serious personal injury or death.

Similarly, if your Air Delivery System or other equipment items have been O_2 cleaned, they too must only come in contact with gases containing oxygen-compatible air. Otherwise they will lose their O_2 service rating. This will be of greatest concern to traveling divers whose equipment comes in contact with air from a wide variety of sources. Some nitrox Divers address this problem by maintaining a second, separate Air Delivery System, intended solely for use with nitrox.

Exercises For the Use of Tables When Planning Nitrox Dives

1. Planning nitrox dives differs most from planning air dives in that when diving with nitrox you must also manage your exposure to _____ .

2. Some nitrox-programmable dive computers not only track a diver's exposure to _____ , they also track a diver's exposure to _____ .

3. Using the SSI Equivalent Air Depth table, determine the equivalent air depth (EAD) for the following depths using EAN32:

Dive 1: 100 ft/30 m. EAD is _____ .

Dive 2: 50 ft/15 m. EAD is _____ .

4. Using the SSI Equivalent Air Depth table and the SSI Doppler No-Decompression Limits table (or the SSI Combined Air/EANx table), determine the Equivalent Air Depth (EAD) and no-decompression limit for a dive to 70 feet/21 metres using EAN32.

The EAD is _____ .

The no-decompression limit is _____ .

5. Using the SSI Equivalent Air Depth table, determine the equivalent air depth (EAD) for the following depths using EAN36:

Dive 1: 90 ft/27 m. EAD is _____ .

Dive 2: 80 ft/24 m. EAD is _____ .

6. Using the SSI Equivalent Air Depth table and the SSI Doppler No-Decompression limits table (or the SSI Combined Air/EANx table), determine the maximum no-decompression limits for the following two dives using EAN36: Dive 1 to 90 ft/27 m followed by a 1:00 surface interval; Dive 2 to 60 ft/18 m. The no-decompression limit for:

Dive No.1 is _____ .

Dive No. 2 is _____ .

7. Use the SSI Equivalent Air Depth table (or the SSI Combined Air/EANx table) to determine the PO_2 for the two dives in question No. 6.

Dive No. 1 PO_2 is _____ .

Dive No. 2 PO_2 is _____ .

8. Using the SSI Combined Air/EANx table, determine the no-decompression limits for an EAN32 dive to 90 ft/27 m that is followed by a 1:00 surface interval and a second dive to 50 ft/15 m. The no-decompression limit for:

Dive No.1 is _____ .

Dive No. 2 is _____ .

9. Using the SSI Combined Air/EANx table, determine the maximum no-decompression limits for the following dives: Dive 1, using EAN36 to 72 ft/22 m followed by a 30 minute surface interval. Dive 2, an air dive to 40 ft/12 m. The no-decompression limit for:

   Dive No.1 is _____ .

   Dive No. 2 is _____ .

10. Using the SSI Combined Air/EANx table, determine the PO_2 for the two dives in Question No. 9.

    Dive No. 1 PO_2 is _____ .

    Dive No. 2 PO_2 is _____ .

11. For added safety, many nitrox divers use a minimum surface interval of _____ between nitrox dives.

12. The term O_2 clean means that all components of the _____ _____ _____ or other equipment items have undergone a _____ _____ _____ designed to remove any trace of _____ _____-_____ , as well as any trace of grease or other non-oxygen-compatible contaminant.

Index

Student
Answer Sheet
Directions

- Transfer your study guide answers to the following four Answer Sheet pages.

- Remember to write your name and the date on each page.

- Sign each page after you have reviewed each incorrect answer with your instructor.

- Your instructor will collect these pages during your SSI Enriched Air Nitrox program.

STUDENT ANSWER SHEET

STUDENT NAME   PART #   DATE

Reviewed and Corrected by Student and Instructor:

STUDENT SIGNATURE   INSTRUCTOR SIGNATURE

1. _____
2. _____
3. _____
4. _____
5. _____
6. _____
7. _____
8. _____
9. _____
10. _____
11. _____
12. _____
13. _____
14. _____
15. _____
16. _____
17. _____
18. _____
19. _____
20. _____

STUDENT ANSWER SHEET

STUDENT NAME   PART #   DATE

Reviewed and Corrected by Student and Instructor:

STUDENT SIGNATURE   INSTRUCTOR SIGNATURE

1. _____
2. _____
3. _____
4. _____
5. _____
6. _____
7. _____
8. _____
9. _____
10. _____
11. _____
12. _____
13. _____
14. _____
15. _____
16. _____
17. _____
18. _____
19. _____
20. _____

STUDENT ANSWER SHEET

STUDENT NAME _____ PART # _____ DATE _____

Reviewed and Corrected by Student and Instructor:

STUDENT SIGNATURE _____ INSTRUCTOR SIGNATURE _____

1. _____
2. _____
3. _____
4. _____
5. _____
6. _____
7. _____
8. _____
9. _____
10. _____
11. _____
12. _____
13. _____
14. _____
15. _____
16. _____
17. _____
18. _____
19. _____
20. _____

STUDENT ANSWER SHEET

STUDENT NAME   PART #   DATE

Reviewed and Corrected by Student and Instructor:

STUDENT SIGNATURE   INSTRUCTOR SIGNATURE

1. _____
2. _____
3. _____
4. _____
5. _____
6. _____
7. _____
8. _____
9. _____
10. _____
11. _____
12. _____
13. _____
14. _____
15. _____
16. _____
17. _____
18. _____
19. _____
20. _____

SSI Program Review Form

Continuous improvement is our goal. Please complete this form.

Program Name/Level_____ Ending Date _____

Instructor Name(s) _____

Overall Program Evaluation: ☐ Excellent ☐ Good ☐ Fair ☐ Poor

What did you like best about the program? _____

_____

What did you like least about the program? _____

_____

Was your exam reviewed by your instructor? ☐ Yes ☐ No

Did you have pool sessions? ☐ Yes ☐ No   Number of pool sessions _____

Did you have open water training dives? ☐ Yes ☐ No

Number of dives for open water training _____ Did you take an exam? ☐ Yes ☐ No

Deepest depth attained during training dives (if applicable) _____

Did you ever feel at any time that your safety was jeopardized? ☐ Yes ☐ No

If yes, please explain. _____

_____

Will you recommend the program to your friends? ☐ Yes ☐ No

What do you suggest to improve the program? _____

_____

Please feel free to use the back of this form for additional comments.

Thank you for helping us develop the
finest possible diver training programs.

If you are pleased with your training and would recommend
it to others, please use the back of this form to provide the names,
addresses, and phone numbers of those who might
be interested in training.

Friend's name _____

Phone number (_____) _____

Address _____

City _____ State _____ Zip _____

Friend's name _____

Phone number (_____) _____

Address _____

City _____ State _____ Zip _____

Comments:

_____

_____

_____

_____

_____

_____

_____

_____

_____

_____

_____

_____

_____

_____

_____

_____

_____